YAËL FARBER: PLAYS ONE

YAËL FARBER

PLAYS ONE

Introduction by
Ingrid Rowland

Molora

Based on *The Oresteia*
by Aeschylus

RAM: The Abduction
of Sita into Darkness

Based on *The Ramayana*
by Valmiki

Mies Julie

Based on *Miss Julie*
by August Strindberg

OBERON BOOKS
LONDON

WWW.OBERONBOOKS.COM

First published in 2015 by Oberon Books Ltd

521 Caledonian Road, London N7 9RH

Tel: +44 (0) 20 7607 3637 / Fax: +44 (0) 20 7607 3629

e-mail: info@oberonbooks.com

www.oberonbooks.com

A catalogue record for this book is available from the British Library.

PB ISBN: 978-1-78319-151-2

E ISBN: 978-1-78319-650-0

Cover design by Konstantinos Vasdekis

Contents

Introduction

Yaël Farber has described her involvement with theatre as a mission. At the heart of her productions, therefore, no matter how dark, there is always a luminous vision to guide characters, actors, and audience forward from the magical rite of performance into a transformed awareness of normal life. Paradoxically, as in these three plays, she draws power from traditional stories and traditional rituals to address contemporary problems head on. Unlike the ancient Greeks, who hid away the most graphic events of tragedy – murder, suicide, rape – Farber shows it all. As a director, she drives the human body to extremes, asking incredible agility of her dancing, leaping, whirling, wrestling actors, pressing their willingness to bare body and soul to the very limits of endurance. She makes comparable demands of her public: we are present to bear witness, to be engaged rather than simply entertained. Each of these plays begins with a warning that production on a proscenium stage will ruin its effect; players and public must meet face to face, on the same level, to recognize their common humanity – and, sadly, inhumanity.

Furthermore, each of these three dramas is based on a classic of dramatic or epic literature transported to a new place and time. *Molora* (2008) sets the ancient Greek saga of the *Oresteia* in contemporary South Africa, with the Commission on Truth and Reconciliation taking the role of the ancient Athenian Court of the Areopagus. *Ram: the Abduction of Sita into Darkness* (2011) recounts a grim episode from the Hindu epic *Ramayana* in connection with a strike by modern Indian sanitation workers. *Mies Julie* (2012) moves August Strindberg's *Fröken Julie* from the midnight sun of a Swedish Midsummer to Freedom Day on an arid South African farmstead. And with each of these transpositions, something remarkable takes place. Rooting these plays in such specific times and such specific settings actually enhances Farber's power, as playwright and director, to draw out their universal qualities. For these great tales, times and continents hardly matter; our similarities as human beings prove stronger than our differences, especially when we gather in a circle to hear a story unfold.

At its origin, the *Oresteia* was a tale of the dying Mediterranean Bronze Age. Agamemnon, the general who led a thousand Greek ships to conquer distant Troy, belonged to the last generation to rule from a series of massive palaces decorated with elaborate frescoes and brimming with gold. Shortly after the Trojan War, between about 1200 and 1100 B.C.E., this palace civilization was destroyed; political systems broke down, writing was lost, Greeks descended into extreme poverty. Memories of that breakdown persist in the story of Agamemnon's homecoming from Troy: his queen, Clytemnestra, has taken a lover during his ten-year absence, and when he finally returns, she kills her husband and abandons their children. Electra, the daughter, descends into bitterness. Their son, Orestes, is bound by tradition to avenge his father's death by slaying the murderer, but that murderer is his own mother. His conflicting obligations potentially make Orestes a monster no matter what he does; significantly, his name means 'mountain man' – he is, by fate and by definition, a kind of savage. All three of the great Greek tragedians, Aeschylus, Sophocles, and Euripides, wrestled with Orestes' dilemma, using it as a way to call for new, more profound forms of justice, aware that their ancestors had created a new civilization, their own, from the ruins of the Bronze Age. In their retellings, Orestes slays his mother, but is tormented by the Furies, his mother's avenging spirits. In his great tragic trilogy, Aeschylus finally turns Orestes over to a court of law, which reaches a split decision. In a spectacular finish, Athena decides to acquit him, but she also gives the Furies a new home and a new cult in Athens.

In *Molora*, the dying Bronze Age becomes the dying system of South African apartheid. Farber replaces the ancient Greek chorus with a chorus of Xhosa women singers. Those ancient Athenians sang melodies and danced, vigorously, in patterns we can only guess at now. But the hypnotic two-tone throat singing of this contemporary chorus creates an ecstatic atmosphere sufficient in itself, one in perfect harmony with the play and with its new South African venue. Aeschylus ended his famous Orestes trilogy of 458 B.C. with a torchlight procession as dusk fell over Athens, knitting up all the unanswered questions of his story with the irrational, energetic rush of pure celebration. The final chorus of *Molora* may be sung in a different language to different instruments than those known to Aeschylus, but the language of bodies in motion knows no borders, and the effect of this South African dance must be no less exhilarating than the memory of that long-ago torchlight parade. Likewise, the sword dance that Orestes performs in *Molora* as he circles around a smoldering altar hews with absolute truth to the spirit of Greek tragedy, not only because tragedy is the stylized product of an ancient circle dance around a burnt sacrifice, but because, in human terms, Orestes needs to work himself into a frenzy before he can contemplate doing what he must do with that sword – namely drive it into his mother. But Farber's most brilliant transformation of the Orestes legend is to have the chorus, as the embodiment of Truth and Reconciliation, stop the murder before it has happened, to hold Orestes to their superior, forgiving justice before he awakens the Furies.

The justice in *Ram*, by contrast, is a bitter justice. The original version of the Hindu epic is thought to date from about the same time as Athenian tragedy, the 5-4th century B.C.E., its 50,000 verses centering on the battles of the virtuous hero Rama against vice in all its various forms. Farber, however, concentrates her attention on the story of Rama's wife Sita, who represents purity and female divinity as Rama himself represents male virtue, and joins him in his battles. When Rama and Sita are living in the forest as exiles from his rightful kingdom, Sita is abducted by Ravana, the monstrous king of Sri Lanka. With the help of his brother and the Monkey God Hanuman, Rama eventually rescues his wife, but he doubts that she can have maintained her purity during her captivity; she finally proves herself by passing through fire. Even after they have been reunited, rumors persist about her, and eventually Rama abandons her (although they reunite again at the end of the *Ramayana*). A televised version of the story was extraordinarily popular in India in 1987-88, so much so that it sparked a strike by sanitation workers across northern India in 1988, who demanded that the federal government commission more episodes of the program. In Farber's retelling, the theatre itself becomes a village gathered around a television set like the Indian audiences in 1987-88, and the discussion of Sita's purity becomes graphically urgent when Ravana not only imprisons Sita, but finally rapes and kills her. Her ravaged physical self appears as a separate 'Sita-body' that takes its own part in the drama; Sita herself, like Rama, is immortal, the human embodiment of a goddess, but this process of psychological removal is well known in real victims of sexual assault. If the Sita-body is violated, then, does this mean that Sita herself is also defiled? Furthermore, as Ravana will discover, his act of violence ultimately turns back on itself without Rama and his armies having to come to the rescue. This retelling of the *Ramayana* holds Rama to a more trenchant definition of virtue than the traditional warrior's prowess, and the loss of Sita is portrayed as an absolute loss to any society that suppresses the feminine side of divinity.

Mies Julie presents an equally harrowing examination of the dynamics between men and women, further complicated by conflicts of race, class, and rootedness in a particular place. Strindberg, in 1888, portrayed a consciously Darwinian struggle between Miss Julie, the countess who represents Sweden's fading aristocracy, and the upward strivings of the valet Jean, in contrast with the long-suffering, pious cook Christine, Jean's fiancée. It is Jean, in the end, who hands Miss Julie the razor with which she will presumably commit suicide offstage, thus ensuring the survival of the fittest. Farber shifts this drama to a South African farm in 2012, where Julie is no longer aristocratic, but simply white; in her own way, then, she is as tough as John, the black servant she has known since childhood and begins to challenge on a hot April 27, when the country stops to celebrate Freedom Day. Soon, of course, we see that true freedom from apartheid is still no more than a distant hope; Julie, John, and his mother Christine are entirely in its thrall. In Strindberg's staging, Jean and Julie withdraw to Jean's room when their flirtation takes a serious turn; here John and Julie copulate, hard, on the kitchen table in front of us. Like Strindberg's couple, Farber's pair dream in their uncomfortable afterglow of starting a hotel together, and in today's world the idea has a plausibility it may not have had in Sweden in 1888. It is all the more shocking, therefore, when John kills Julie's pet bird as useless extra baggage; apartheid has brutalized him as much as it has brutalized Julie at her most imperious. For her part, Christine, obsessed with the presence of her ancestors buried beneath the foundations of the house, brings on a searching discussion of who truly belongs to the soil of South Africa; for Julie's ancestors lie buried there as well. Ultimately, it is this very sense of rootedness that destroys the brief dream that John and Julie spin of running off together, and when Julie kills herself – as she does, again, before our eyes – it is with a farm implement, a sickle, driven into her womb, which came so close to fostering the mixed-race children of a new South Africa. It is impossible to come away from *Ram* or *Mies Julie* without feeling that the world must change; *Molora* points the way. Yaël Farber's theatre will leave no participant unmoved.

MOLORA

Foreword

by Yael Farber, Director and Adaptor

'This thing called reconciliation... If I am understanding it correctly...if it means this perpetrator, this man who has killed my son, if it means he becomes human again, this man, so that I, so that all of us, get our humanity back...then I agree, then I support it all.'

Cynthia Ngwenyu, mother of one of the murdered Gugulethu 7, when facing her son's state-sanctioned murderer at the TRC

In the aftermath of South Africa's transition into democracy in 1994, the world held its collective breath in anticipation of a civil war that would surely unleash the rage of generations shattered by the Apartheid regime. South Africa defied expectations, however, lighting the way forward for all nations trapped in quagmires of revenge. Despite the praise Nelson Mandela received from 'First World' leaders for heralding great restraint through this transition in our troubled land, nothing could convince those same leaders to check their own ancient eye-for-an-eye, knee-jerk response and their resulting offensives of 'Shock and Awe' on the women and children of Baghdad. South Africa's relatively peaceful transformation was an extraordinary exception in our vengeful world

But such a journey is neither simple nor easy, and has little to do with the reductive notions of a miraculously forgiving Rainbow Nation or 'turning the other cheek'. In the epic eye of South Africa's storm, it was not the gods – nor any *deus ex machina* – that delivered us from ourselves. It was the common everyman and everywoman who, in the years following democracy, gathered in modest halls across the country to face their perpetrators across a table, and find a way forward for us all.

The ancient *Oresteia* trilogy tells the story of the rightful heirs to the House of Atreus, dispossessed of their inheritance. Forced to live as a servant in the halls of her own father's house, Elektra waits for her brother Orestes to return from exile to the land of his ancestors and take back what is rightfully theirs. The premise of this ancient story was striking to me as a powerful canvas on which to explore the history of dispossession, violence and human-rights violations in the country I grew up in. I had long been interested in creating a work that explores the journey back from the dark heart of unspeakable trauma and pain – and the choices facing those shattered by the past.

Molora is an examination of the spirals of violence begat by vengeance, and the breaking of such cycles by the ordinary man.

In the long nights following the devastating attack on the World Trade Centre, amid the grief, recriminations and the Bush administration's indiscriminate wielding of revenge, a fine white powdery substance gently floated down upon heart-broken New York.

Our story begins with a handful of cremated remains that Orestes delivers to his mother's door…

From the ruins of Hiroshima, Baghdad, Palestine, Northern Ireland, Rwanda, Bosnia, the concentration camps of Europe and modern-day Manhattan – to the remains around the fire after the storytelling is done…

Molora (the Sesotho word for 'ash') is the truth we must all return to, regardless of what faith, race or clan we hail from.

The Ngqoko Cultural Group

The Chorus Reinvented

The Ngqoko Cultural Group is a body of men and women committed to the indigenous music, songs and traditions of the rural Xhosa communities. Hailing from the humble rural town of Lady Frere in South Africa, the group was first formed in 1980. A single bow player and her daughter were maintaining the practice of playing music together, when a German visitor, Dawie Dargie, began working with the Xhosa musicians with the help of Tsolwana Mpayipheli as translator. In 1983 Mpayipheli, or 'Teacher' as he is respectfully known, discovered several other musicians who joined the group. They have since established a reputation as guardians of the rural Xhosa culture, maintaining the survival and presence of indigenous South African music and instruments.

In *Molora* the device of the ancient Greek Chorus is radically reinvented in the form of a deeply traditional, rural Xhosa aesthetic. Farber chose to collaborate with The Ngqoko Cultural Group with the intention of rediscovering the original power of the device of the Chorus in ancient Greek theatre. In her quest to find a group that could represent the weight and conscience of the community – as she believes is the Chorus' purpose – she happened upon the unearthly sound of the Ngqoko Group's UMNGQOKOLO (Split-Tone Singing).

Farber drove out to the rural Transkei to meet with the women, where she told them the story of the *Oresteia*. The reaction to the story was deeply felt and met with much discussion on the moral implication of killing your own mother. Farber instantly knew she had found the Chorus to this new *Oresteia*.

Trained in this ancient art of singing, these women have been taught from an early age, the skill of creating this vocal phenomenon, as well as being masters of the ancient musical instruments that are an intrinsic part of their everyday lives in the rural Transkei. The mouth bows, calabash bows, mouth harps and milking drums form an array of traditional musical instruments that they – as Chorus – play in accompaniment to the text of *Molora*. The sounds of these unique

Xhosa artists lend a haunting texture of sound, which is unfamiliar to most modern ears, and evokes a deeply emotional accompaniment to the work.

The envisaging of the Chorus as a group of 'ordinary' African women provides the context of the Truth Commission, which witnessed thousands of such 'ordinary' folk gathering in halls across South Africa to hear the details of a loved one's death at the hands of the State.

The individuals that constitute The Ngqoko Cultural Group represent, in this context, the unique grace and dignity that was evident in the common man who chose a different path for South Africa. Within the Ngqoko group are two spiritual diviners who are trained in the channelling of ancestral powers. While these women are restrained in their use of authentic trance on stage, their authority in spiritual conduct allows a moment in which the audience may experience a deep participation in a prayer to our ancestors for an end to the cycle of violence in South Africa – and indeed the world.

Acknowledgements

- **Yana Sakelaris** for her dramaturgical contributions and assistance when adapting the text

- **The Ngqoko Cultural Group** for their songs, praises and traditional practices which profoundly shaped this work

- **Bongeka Mongwana** for her Xhosa Translations

- Past and current cast members, with whom *Molora* grew and continues to grow

- This work was first made possible by **Standard Bank National Festival of the Arts**

MOLORA

Dedicated to Lindiwe Chibi, *Molora*'s original Elektra

Your light continues to shine for us all

A Note on the Quotations

The patchwork of quotations from the original Greek plays used in *Molora* are flagged up in the footnotes: where the translations are known they are identified with initials (see below); where I have been unable to rediscover the original version I quoted from, the references are followed by (SU), ie 'source unknown'. The known sources are:

Aeschylus, *Agamemnon*
>   LM: Louis MacNeice (Faber, 1967)
>   RF: Robert Fagles (Penguin, 1977)

Aeschylus, *The Libation Bearers* (*Choephoroi*)
>   IJ: Ian Johnston (http://www.mala.bc.ca/~Johnstoi/aeschylus/
>   libationbearers.htm) [line numbers refer to the translation]

Sophocles, *Electra*
>   RCJ: Richard Claverhouse Jebb
>   (http://classics.mit.edu/Sophocles/electra.html)
>   DG: David Grene, from Grene and Lattimore, eds, *The*
>   *Complete Greek Tragedies* (University of Chicago Press, 1957)

Euripides, *Electra*
>   ECP: Edward Paley Coleridge
>   (http://classics.mit.edu/Euripides/electra_eur.html)

The line numbers of the Greek text are given in square brackets at the end of the footnotes. These are taken from the following Loeb Classical Library parallel editions of the relevant texts: *Aeschylus*, vol II (William Heinemann, 1957); *Sophocles*, vol II (William Heinemann, 1961); *Euripides*, vol III (Harvard University Press, 1998).

Characters

KLYTEMNESTRA

ELEKTRA

ORESTES

CHORUS OF WOMEN
&
TRANSLATOR

The first British performance of *Molora* was at the Barbican Centre on 9 April 2008, in a production by the Farber Foundry in association with Oxford Playhouse (originally produced in association with The Market Theatre, Johannesburg). The cast was as follows:

KLYTEMNESTRA, Dorothy Ann Gould

ELEKTRA, Jabulile Tshabalala

ORESTES, Sandile Matsheni

CHORUS & MUSICIANS, The Ngqoko Cultural Group:
Nofenishala Mvotyo, Nogcinile Yekani, Nokhaya Mvotyo, Nopasile Mvotyo, Nosomething Ntese, Tandiwe Lungisa, Tsolwana B Mpayipheli

Creator and Director Yael Farber

Assistant Director and Dramaturgical Contributor
Yana Sakelaris

Vernacular Text Translators Current and past cast members

Instrument and Song Arrangements The Ngqoko Cultural Group

Set Designers Larry Leroux and Leigh Colombick

Costume Designers Natalie Lundon and Johny Mathole

Lighting Supervisor Paul Peyton Moffitt

mise en scène

This work should never be played on a raised stage behind a
proscenium arch, but on the floor to a raked audience. If being
presented in a traditional theatre, the audience should be seated on
stage with the action, preferably with all drapes and theatre curtains
stripped from the stage and the audience in front of, left and right
of the performance. Contact with the audience must be immediate
and dynamic, with the audience complicit – experiencing the story
as witnesses or participants in the room, rather than as voyeurs
excluded from yet looking in on the world of the story.

The ideal venue is a bare hall or room – much like the drab, simple
venues in which most of the testimonies were heard during the course
of South Africa's Truth and Reconciliation Commission: Two large,
old tables – each with a chair – face one another on opposite ends of
the playing space. Beneath Klytemnestra's testimony table is a large
bundle wrapped in black plastic. Upon each table is a microphone on
a stand. Between these two tables is a low platform which demarcates
the area in which the past / memory will be re-enacted. Centre of this
platform is a grave filled with the red sand of Africa. Beside it lies an
old pickaxe. Neither the grave nor murder weapon can be seen when
the audience enters – as the platform is initially covered with a large
industrial sheet of black plastic.

Along the back of the playing area, upstage and facing the audience,
are seven empty, austere-looking chairs, upon which the **CHORUS**
of **WOMEN** – who will come to hear the testimonies – will sit. The
audience is seated in front of and around the performance area, as
if incorporated into the testimonies. They are the community that
provides the context to this event. Seated amongst audience members
are the seven **CHORUS** members, as well as **KLYTEMNESTRA** and
ELEKTRA.

prologue

As the audience wait for the play to begin, an elderly Xhosa woman emerges from the audience, and moves in silence into the performance area. She is dressed with the modesty characteristic of rural women from the Transkei. She has clay on her face and a blanket about her shoulders. She walks over the platform and considers the space. Holding a corner of the plastic sheet which covers the platform – she gently begins to gather it towards her. In the silence, the plastic drags away to reveal a richly-toned, earthen floor. The performance space, now fully visible, has a bleak beauty. In the centre of this earthen floor is the grave. The woman seats herself beside the mound of red soil, picks up her traditional calabash bow and begins the ancient singular sound of the UHADI (Calabash Bow). She sings softly in Xhosa:

Ho laphalal'igazi.

[BLOOD HAS BEEN SPILT HERE.]

*One by one, the other **WOMEN** of the **CHORUS** rise gently from the audience, and move towards the stage, joining the song. All are dressed simply, with blankets around their shoulders. The last member of the **CHORUS** is a man in a hat and old suit. They take their places on the chairs upstage and continue singing. **KLYTEMNESTRA** – a white woman in middle age – rises from the audience, crosses the playing space and takes her place at one of the wooden tables. She is here to testify. **ELEKTRA** – a young, black woman – follows, and sits at the opposite table. Perpetrator and victim face one another at last. The **CHORUS** concludes its song. in silence, the UHADI (Calabash Bow) is passed quietly down the line of **CHORUS** members, and laid on the ground. The silence* *ensues – lasting almost a minute. Everyone waits without emotion or movement. Finally, **KLYTEMNESTRA** pulls the live microphone towards her. An ominous sound fills the room, as it scrapes along the wooden table. The neon lights above the tables and **CHORUS** flicker on. The Hearings have begun.*

i: testimony

KLYTEMNESTRA: ¹A great ox –
                  As they say –
                  Stands on my tongue.

*As she begins to speak – the **CHORUS** all turn their heads to
the right, to listen to her.*

TRANSLATOR: Ndise ndayinkukhw' isikw'umlomo.
                  [A GREAT OX...
                  AS THEY SAY...
                  STANDS ON MY TONGUE.]

KLYTEMNESTRA: ²The house itself, if it took voice, could
                  tell the case most clearly. But I will only
                  speak to those who know.
                  For the others – I remember nothing.

She pauses before her testimony. It is hard for her to speak.

                  ³Here I stand and here I struck
                  and here my work is done.
                  I did it all. I don't deny it.
                  No.
                  He had no way to flee or fight his
                  destiny –
                  our never-ending, all-embracing net.
                  I cast it wide.

---

1   The Watchman in *Agamemnon* (LM), p 14 [36]

2   The Watchman in *Agamemnon* (LM), p 14 [36]

3   Adapted from Clytemnestra in *Agamemnon* (RF), ll 1398–1415, p 161
[1379–1392]

I coil him round and round in the robes
of doom... And then I strike him once,
twice, and at each stroke he cries in
agony.
He buckles at the knees and crashes here!
And when he's down I add the third –
the final blow,
to the god who saves the dead beneath
the ground.
I send that blow home…
in homage…
like a prayer.
So he goes down, and the life is bursting
out of him - great sprays of blood.
And the murderous shower wounds me,
dyes me black.
And I… I revel like the Earth
when the spring rains come down.
The blessed gifts of God.
And the new green spear splits the sheath
and rips to birth in glory!
[4]Here lies Agamemnon my husband
made a corpse by this right hand.
A Masterpiece of Justice.
Done is done.

TRANSLATOR: Kugqityiwe.
[DONE IS DONE.]

---

4   *Agamemnon* (RF), ll 1429–31, p 162 [1395–6]

ELEKTRA – who has been listening silently – draws the live microphone towards her. We hear it scrape slowly along the rough table top.

ELEKTRA: Ndingasiqala ngaphi isicengcelezo sam ngenkohlakalo yakho?

[5][WITH WHICH OF YOUR EVILS SHALL I BEGIN MY RECITAL?]

Kona, ndingayeka phi na?

[WITH WHICH SHALL I END IT?]

Zange ndayeka ukuyilungiselela into endandiya kuyithetha ebusweni bakho…

[I HAVE NEVER CEASED TO REHEARSE WHAT I WOULD TELL YOU TO YOUR FACE…]

If ever I were freed from my old terrors. And now I am. So I pay you back with these words I could not utter before: You were my ruin…

Kodwa ndingakwenzanga nto.

[YET I HAD DONE NOTHING TO YOU.]

You poisoned me with your deeds. You are the shadow that fell on my life and made a child of me through fear. I have hated you so long…

And now you want to look into my heart? You who did this to my father will pay.

[6]For if the dead lie in dust and nothingness,

while the guilty pay not with blood for blood –

---

5   Adapted from *Electra* (Euripides: EPC) [907–8]

6   Adapted from *Electra* (Sophocles: RCJ) [245–6]

> Then we are nothing but history without
> a future.

*The **CHORUS** breaks into UMNGQOKOLO (Split-Tone
Singing – the powerful, ancient form of 'throat singing'
that traditional Xhosa women train in from an early age).
KLYTEMNESTRA and **ELEKTRA** slowly rise from their
chairs, maintaining eye contact. They move out from behind
the safety of their tables and square up on the periphery, at
opposite ends of the raised earthen floor.
In a decisive moment, they step onto the earthen floor. With
this gesture, mother and daughter commit to the process
of unearthing the past. **ELEKTRA** pulls her dress down to
expose her back and shoulders. **KLYTEMNESTRA** receives
a pot of hot water and cloth from one of the **WOMEN** of the
CHORUS.*

ii: murder

***ELEKTRA** is a child of seven years. Her mother washes her
with the steaming water from the pot. **ELEKTRA** sings softly
to herself, over the sound of the UMNGQOKOLO (Split-Tone
Singing) which will continue throughout the following scene:*

ELEKTRA: (*Singing.*)

> One man went to plough
> Went to plough the mielies
> One man went to plough
> Went to plough the mielies
> Two men went to plough…

KLYTEMNESTRA wraps ELEKTRA in a blanket, embraces her as though in farewell, and then rises with determination. She grabs the end of the pickaxe that lies on the ground. She drags it behind her, in a trance. It scrapes audibly along the wooden platform. She heads towards her testimony table.

ELEKTRA: Mama…uyaphi?
                  [MAMA…..WHERE ARE YOU GOING?]
                  Mama…mama…?
                  Uyaphi Mama? [WHERE MAMA?]

KLYTEMNESTRA climbs onto the table with the axe raised high above her head. She screams, and slams the axe onto the table. With this blow, she has struck her husband – Agamemnon – dead. She squats on the table and, scooping from an enamel bowl, covers her expressionless face, arms and hands in blood. She jumps from the table, and pulls at the plastic bundle hidden there. The body of Agamemnon – played by the actor who will perform the part of ORESTES – is revealed. ELEKTRA screams.

ELEKTRA: Mama yintoni le uyenzileyo?
                  [MAMA WHAT HAVE YOU DONE?]
                  (*Running to her father's body and flinging
                  herself onto it.*) Tata uyandibona na?
                  Uyandibona Tata?
                  [DADDY CAN YOU SEE ME? CAN YOU SEE ME
                  DADDY?]

KLYTEMNESTRA pulls her daughter off her dead husband. ELEKTRA fights her way back to the body several times. KLYTEMNESTRA throws her from it brutally.

KLYTEMNESTRA: Don't look!

*The **CHORUS** concludes their UMNGQOKOLO (Split-Tone Singing).*
*In the silence we hear **KLYTEMNESTRA** panting with effort. She drags the body towards the grave and begins to bury him in the soil. A **WOMAN** of the **CHORUS** plays ISITOLO-TOLO (Jew's Harp) as the actor rolls away and rises slowly, leaving **KLYTEMNESTRA** to finish covering where she has concealed the corpse. He recedes and exits, dragging behind him the black plastic he was wrapped in, and a trail of dust in the air. **ELEKTRA** grasps the other end of this plastic as though to hold him earthbound, but is forced to release him as he disappears. **KLYTEMNESTRA** moves to the pot of water and methodically begins to wash the blood from her arms, hands and face. **ELEKTRA** crawls to her father's grave.*

ELEKTRA: (*Screaming in grief.*) PAPAAAAA!!!!

KLYTEMNESTRA: [7]Here I stand…
                  And here I struck…
                  And here my work is done!

*She throws the bloodied cloth into the pot of water, with force. The water spills over the sides of the Pot. The **CHORUS** sings in UMNGQOKOLO (Split-Tone Singing).*

---

7   *Agamemnon* (RF), ll 1396–9, p 161 [1379–80]

iii: exile

*The **TRANSLATOR** of the **CHORUS** walks across
the platform with the UHADI (Calabash Bow) and
sits on the downstage right corner. A woman from the
CHORUS seats herself on the upstage left corner behind
the UMASENGWANA (Milking / Friction Drum). As the
UMNGQOKOLO (Split Tone) singing resolves, the UHADI
(Calabash Bowing) begins. **ELEKTRA** moves centre stage
and addresses the audience directly.*

ELEKTRA: It is seventeen years since she hacked my
father like a tree with an axe.
Wapharhaza intloko kaTata kubini
ngezembe echitha ubuchopho bakhe
emhlabeni.
[HACKED HIS HEAD IN TWO WITH AN AXE – AND
SPILT HIS BRAINS ONTO THE SOIL.]
Split his face open with an axe and buried
his body on the outskirts of the village. I
saw her and Ayesthus – her lover – dance
in his blood that night.
I tried to help him – but I was only a
child.
'Tata [FATHER] can you see me? Can you see
me Tata [FATHER]? Please say yes.'
I stole my little brother Orestes from his
bed that night.

KLYTEMNESTRA: (*Looking frantically in the empty blanket
beside the pot.*)
Orestes?… Orestes?

35

ELEKTRA: I knew they would kill him too, for his birthright, if I did not send him away.

ELEKTRA pulls the blanket from her shoulders and rolls into a small bundle. This is her infant brother ORESTES – stolen from his bed.

(*Calling urgently into the dark.*)
Mama Nosomething? Mama Nosomething...

One of the women of the CHORUS – Ma NOSOMETHING – stands at the corner of the playing area.

Ma NOSOMETHING: Ngubani lo undibizayo?
[WHO CALLS ME?]

ELEKTRA: Ndim, ndicela undincede undithathele lo'mtwana toro, umkhulise ngathi ngowakho.
[IT IS ME. PLEASE HELP ME! TAKE THIS CHILD FAR FROM HERE AND RAISE HIM LIKE YOUR OWN.]

Ma NOSOMETHING: Kulungile mntwana wam ndizakumthatha Ndimkhulise de abemmdala.
[ALRIGHT MY CHILD. I WILL TAKE HIM FROM HERE AND RAISE HIM UNTIL HE IS GROWN.]

Ma NOSOMETHING steals away into the dark and returns to the other WOMEN of the CHORUS, who gather around the 'child', kissing and touching the bundle.

ELEKTRA: I gave him to the women of our Tribe to
            grow him like a tree in the mountains,
            until he became a man.
            For seventeen years I did not see him.
            I had to live with her.
            I was the wall she beat against every day.

The sound of UMASENGWANA (Milking / Friction Drum),
as KLYTEMNESTRA pushes ELEKTRA's face into the pot of
water she used to wash her as a child.

iv: interrogation

KLYTEMNESTRA: Where is he?

She pulls her from the water after a long moment.

                Where is my baby?
                What have you done with my boy?

ELEKTRA will not give her mother the information she is
seeking. KLYTEMNESTRA pushes her face beneath the
water once again. ELEKTRA endures the interrogation with
a courage reminiscent of a political resistance fighter.
KLYTEMNESTRA turns from ELEKTRA and lights a
cigarette.

                [8]And Ham saw the nakedness of his
                father, and told his brethren without. And

---

8   Book of Genesis 9:20–27. The 'curse of Ham' has been used by some to
justify racism, systems like Apartheid, and the enslavement of people of Black
African ancestry – believed to be descendants of Ham.

Shem and Japheth went backward; and
their faces were backward, so that they
saw not their father's nakedness. And
when he awoke from his wine, and knew
what his younger child had done unto
him. He said…

(*Reaching out for ELEKTRA's hand.*)
Cursed be your children.

She pushes the burning tip of the cigarette into ELEKTRA's
palm. ELEKTRA screams.

The servants of servants shall they be
unto their brethren. The seed of your
line shall be the carriers of water and the
hewers of wood.

Straddling ELEKTRA, she pushes the burning tip into the
side of her daughter's neck.
Screaming, ELEKTRA tries to crawl away.

For the Lord thy God is a jealous God.
And your dark descendents shall live in
slavery… All the days of their lives.
What have you done with my baby?

Exploding with rage at ELEKTRA's silence.

WHERE IS MY SON?

ELEKTRA, though weeping, will not relent.
KLYTEMNESTRA gathers her from the floor and cradles her
daughter.

(*With grim determination.*)
I'll get it out of you.

v: dreams

*KLYTEMNESTRA stands and walks towards her
Testimony Table. She puts out her cigarette as the sound of
UMASENGWANA (Milking / Friction Drum) fades. She
seats herself to testify. She speaks into the mike, directly to
audience.*

KLYTEMNESTRA: What is guilt?
                 What is memory?
                 What is pain?
                 Things that wake me in the night…
                 By day I stand by what I have done
                 But at night I dream –
                 And dreams don't lie.

*She climbs slowly onto the Testifying Table – which has now
become her bed. She is tormented, twisting in her slumber.
Three WOMEN of the CHORUS rise from their seats. They
move towards her humming an ancient lullaby.*

ELEKTRA: (*Addressing the audience directly.*)
                 I would hear her through the walls each
                 night…
                 [9]Dreaming she was giving birth –

---

9   Adapted from *The Libation Bearers* (IJ), l 660 [527]

39

*The **WOMEN** from the **CHORUS** are the attendant
midwives to **KLYTEMNESTRA**. They help her into a
squatting position, supporting her from behind.*

MIDWIVES: Pusha! Pusha! [PUSH! PUSH!]

ELEKTRA: But from her womb comes a snake.

*One of the midwives pulls a writhing, blood-covered snake
from between **KLYTEMNESTRA**'s legs. They place it on her
breast.*

The midwives wrap it in a blanket and
put it on her breast.
But with her milk it sucks out clots of her
blood.

*KLYTEMNESTRA screams and starts awake. The house is
quiet.*

vi: grief

*ELEKTRA rolls away from the 'wall' through which she was
listening to KLYTEMNESTRA's dream. She stands beside
her father's grave.*

ELEKTRA: The years pass –
and the grass grows over the grave of a
loved one. They told me I was caught in
grief.
People said I must just move on.
But how? How could I forget?

How can we move on until the debt is
paid?

ELEKTRA crawls towards her father's grave and lies upon it.

I would hear them at night from my
father's grave.
The voices of the dead whispering
through the years:

*The **CHORUS** softly sings.*

'Restore my house.'
'The perpetrator has no right to live
between those walls.'
'Take back what is rightfully ours.'
Somewhere out there was my brother in
exile. But until he returned I could do
nothing…but wait.

*The **CHORUS** stands and begins a slow dance, circling
ELEKTRA on her father's grave. They seat themselves along
the periphery of the performance space, watching her.*

Kuni nina Zinyanya zakowethu – nina
ningasekhoyo kulomhlaba – Nina
ningasaboniyo ngaliso lanyama…
[TO YOU MY ANCESTORS – YOU WHO ARE NO
LONGER IN THIS WORLD – YOU WHO SEE THINGS
THAT ARE NOT SEEN…]
It is dark. Light my way.
Nini kuphela enaziyo eyona nto
eyenzekayo.

41

[IT IS YOU ALONE WHO KNOW WHAT TRULY
HAPPENED.]

Send to me – Orestes – my brother – my
blood. Bring him back from exile after
these seventeen years – for
[10]I have no more strength to bear up
alone against the weight of this.

*She nestles into the dark soil of her father's grave, and falls
asleep there.*

vii: grave

*UMASENGWANA (the Milking / Friction Drum) begins
its haunting tempo. KLYTEMNESTRA stands over
Agamemnon's grave – watching ELEKTRA, asleep in
the cemetery soil. KLYTEMNESTRA holds a 'sjambok'
(traditional South African whip made of cured leather). She
cracks the whip. ELEKTRA scrambles from the grave – away
from her mother's quiet, vicious rage.*

KLYTEMNESTRA:	*(Softly, with danger.)* Have you been here all night again? Sleeping on that grave?
ELEKTRA:	Wenza ntoni? [WHAT ARE YOU DOING HERE?] You have no right to be here!

---

10   *Electra* (Sophocles: RCJ) [119–20]

KLYTEMNESTRA: [11]You dare speak to me like this – for my husband is not here to keep you from blaming me and straying out of bounds. You come here although you know your father and I have strictly forbidden it.

ELEKTRA: He is not my father.
Ndiyamoyika. Andimhloniphi
[I FEAR HIM. I DO NOT RESPECT HIM.]
[12]Why do you encourage his violence against me?

KLYTEMNESTRA: It is his way. You too have a stubborn nature!

ELEKTRA: Stubborn because I grieve the father I loved?

KLYTEMNESTRA: Seventeen years you have grieved!
The only thing you love is misery.

ELEKTRA: [13]Only a fool forgets a father's death.

KLYTEMNESTRA: Your father! Always your father Agamemnon! Nothing else lives in you but the death he got from me. But I had an ally in this- [14]for justice slew him, and not I alone. If you were a mother – you would have done the same. This brutal

---

11   *Electra* (Sophocles: SU) [622]

12   Adapted from *Electra* (Euripides: EPC) [1116]

13   *Electra* (Sophocles: SU) [144]

14   *Electra* (Sophocles: RCJ) [528]

father of yours, whom you mourn and
mourn, sacrificed your sister –
For some godforsaken Holy War!
He let her die.
[15]He the begetter only with his seed.
For he did not toil for her for nine long
months as I did
– The mother that bore her.

ELEKTRA: It was War! He had no choice.

KLYTEMNESTRA: We all have choice. And I made mine.
I took what was owed me:
Breath for breath, and life for life.
[16]And so would say your dead sister, if
she could speak.
[17]Let Agamemnon make no great boasts
in the halls of Hell. For he has paid for
what he first began.

ELEKTRA: Ngamthetho wuphi? [BY WHAT LAW?]

KLYTEMNESTRA: By the justice of a mother.

ELEKTRA: Were Orestes and I not also born of your
womb?
My brother would have died too by your
lover's hand that night, if I had not sent
him away.

---

15   Adapted from *Electra* (Sophocles: DG), ll 534–5, p 146 [533]

16   *Electra* (Sophocles: SU) [548]

17   Clytemnestra in *Agamemnon* (SU) [1528–9]

And now all these years I am forced to
serve in the Halls of my Father's House.
Is my dead sister the only one to know
your Justice as a mother?

KLYTEMNESTRA: [18]She begged him: 'Do not kill me before
my time. Don't force me to gaze at
darkness in the world below.'

ELEKTRA: It was the price of war.

KLYTEMNESTRA: Until you have borne a child – don't you
dare talk to me about the price of war.

ELEKTRA: Yes! My womb remains empty and I am
without child.
The man who sleeps in my father's bed
has forbidden any man to come near me
– for fear that I will breed a son who will
some day avenge my father's death.
But Agamemnon's line will not die.
My brother lives.
Seventeen years ago – he was a child. But
time passes.
And the boy is now a man.

KLYTEMNESTRA: A man? And where is this man who
promises to come…
But never resolves.

ELEKTRA: He will come!
Uyazi ukuba uza kuza [YOU KNOW HE WILL!]

---

18   Iphigenia to Agamemnon. Euripides, *Iphigenia in Aulis* (SU) [1219]

	And you fear it.
	Every night you wait for his shadow to fall over your bed. You are dreaming of him again….
KLYTEMNESTRA:	(*Startled.*) Who told you that?
ELEKTRA:	I hear your fear at night through the walls.
	I see you coming to pay penance each year at your victim's grave? You think no one knows you.
	But I see your heart.
	I know it hurts.
KLYTEMNESTRA:	I am done here. (*Turning to go.*)
ELEKTRA:	You loved me once, I think.
	You loved my brother – and you loved me…

ELEKTRA starts to weep. KLYTEMNESTRA falters for a moment.

	Mama, if I speak gently – can I say my truth?
KLYTEMNESTRA:	(*Casting aside her 'sjambok' and coming to her.*)
	[19]Indeed, you have my leave.

---

19   *Electra* (Sophocles: RCJ) [556–7]

And if you always addressed me in such a
gentle tone, you would be heard without
pain.

ELEKTRA grasps her legs, kneeling before her.

ELEKTRA: I want only to know you.
                    Who you were before the hurting...
                    who we could have been.

KLYTEMNESTRA: [20]I am not so exceeding glad at the deeds
                    that I have done...

ELEKTRA: I know. And I know you wish it could
                    have been different, but you breed with
                    him, and honor his line, while you cast us
                    out - your true children.
                    Yonke lento uyenzela isiqu sakho – Hayi
                    intombi yakho ebuleweyo!
                    [ALL OF THIS YOU ARE DOING FOR YOURSELF – NOT
                    FOR YOUR MURDERED DAUGHTER!]
                    Taking night after night...the man who
                    has my father's blood on his hands –
                    Kule nyo yakho! [INTO YOUR CUNT!]
                    You are nothing but that man's Bitch.

KLYTEMNESTRA, enraged, charges at ELEKTRA with
the whip. ELEKTRA runs in terror and hides behind the
CHORUS of WOMEN. They raise their arms to protect her,
and she huddles behind them. KLYTEMNESTRA speaks to
all.

---

20 *Electra* (Euripides: EPC) [1106]

KLYTEMNESTRA: Let me tell you about this Bitch – and how she met the man you call father. There are things you do not know about me child: A history that was written long before you were born.

I too was happy once.

I was not always Klytemnestra who carried this curse.

Before your father – I was married to a man I loved – with a child – my first born.

The power in that bond you will never know.

A woman giving birth is an animal in pain.

Hurt her child – and the wound is hers… Cuts her where she cannot heal.

I met your father the day he opened up my first husband and ripped out his guts. [21]He tore this – my firstborn from my breast. Then holding the child by its new ankles – he smashed its tiny head against a rock. Then took me for his wife.

Ah! My daughter, he that begat you murdered more than one of my children. For well you know – years later he would slit your own sister's throat as a sacrifice for peace.

PEACE? WHOSE PEACE?

It is an old and terrible world, and I feel its pain.

---

21   Source unknown

But if you ever dare speak to me like that
again,
I will answer you from my black heart.
For it is not I who first taught you to be
so base.

ELEKTRA: [22]Base deeds are taught by base.
                 If you find me accomplished in such
                 things…
                 It is because I am my mother's daughter.

KLYTEMNESTRA: [23]I and my deeds give you too much
                 matter for words.

ELEKTRA: [24]The words are thine – not mine.
                 For yours is the act – and the act finds its
                 utterance.

KLYTEMNESTRA: I have lived a long time my daughter.
                 Eye for an eye, blood for blood, and a
                 tooth for a tooth.
                 It is and will always be men's only truth.

*Suddenly, ELEKTRA grabs the 'sjambok' from
KLYTEMNESTRA's hand.*

ELEKTRA: (*With danger.*)
                 [25]Take care in making such a law for men,
                 that you not make trouble for yourself.

---

22   *Electra* (Sophocles: RCJ) [621]

23   *Electra* (Sophocles: RCJ) [622–3]

24   *Electra* (Sophocles: RCJ) [624–5]

25   Adapted from *Electra* (Sophocles: RCJ) [581–2]

> For, if we are to take blood for blood,
> then by that law… Wena! [YOU]

In an open threat, she points at her with the 'sjambok'.

> You would be the first to die.

*Mother and daughter stare at each other. The danger is
now out in the open. KLYTEMNESTRA turns her back on
ELEKTRA, as the WOMEN break into UMNGQOKOLO
(Split-Tone Singing). KLYTEMNESTRA walks away and
ELEKTRA watches her, standing her ground.*

viii: wet bag method

*KLYTEMNESTRA moves centre stage with her chair raised,
upside down, above her head. The effect is of an animal
with horns, under threat. She turns the chair, places it and
sits. ELEKTRA walks to the table, sits and speaks into the
microphone, directly to her perpetrator.*

ELEKTRA: (*Testimony.*) Years passed between us.
        Mother and daughter.
        But I was not permitted to sit at the table.
        You fed me like a dog.
        I was a servant in the halls of my father's
        house.
        No-one ever talks about the night you
        spilled my father's blood.
        It is as though the past never happened.
        But a daughter remembers.

Sisiyatha sodwa esingalibala ukubulawa
kuka tata waso.

[ONLY A FOOL WOULD FORGET HER FATHER'S
MURDER.]

Every day you tried to break my strength.
Everyday you tried to destroy my spirit.

*She comes out from behind her table and stands before a
seated* **KLYTEMNESTRA**.

Please, demonstrate for this commission
how you tried to get information out of
me as to my brother's whereabouts.

ELEKTRA *turns her back to* **KLYTEMNESTRA** *and lies,
belly down, in front of her.* **KLYTEMNESTRA** *moves to*
ELEKTRA *and straddles her. She takes a plastic bag from her
pocket, places it over* **ELEKTRA**'*s head, and pulls it tightly.*
ELEKTRA *begins to suffocate.*
*This form of torture should be a direct visual reference to the
'Wet Bag Method' – graphically demonstrated at the Truth
Commission, and used by South African Security Police to
torture political activists during the Apartheid regime's rule.
This suffocation should be performed for longer than the
audience would be comfortable with. As* **ELEKTRA** *starts
to lose consciousness, and her desperate kicking fades –*
KLYTEMNESTRA *suddenly pulls the bag from her head.*
ELEKTRA *gasps for breath.*

(*Sobbing with rage.*)
One day you will face your God. And
ask forgiveness for the things you did in
those years…

KLYTEMNESTRA: There was so much fear in those years.
Every night the shadow of my son would
fall over my bed.
The inevitable vengeance he would one
day bring.
For those we harm as children –
Grow up to be men.

ix: initiation

*The CHORUS, in full voice, sings the traditional song
for young Xhosa men returning from their initiation in
the mountains. ORESTES is wrapped, and with his face
shrouded, in the striking white and red initiate's blanket,
holding a stick over his shoulder. He moves with slow grace
towards the centre of the performance area. The CHORUS
seat themselves in a circle around ORESTES. The WOMAN
who took him, as an infant from ELEKTRA, steps forward to
praise him and offer the traditional WORDS OF WISDOM.*

WOMAN: [26]Uyindoda ngoku, hamba
uyokukhathalela udade wenu.
[NOW THAT YOU ARE A MAN – GO AND TAKE CARE
OF YOUR SISTER.]
Hamba uyokwenza izinto zobudoda.
[GO AND DO MANLY THINGS.]
Hamba uyokukhathalela usapho lwakho.
[GO AND TAKE CARE OF YOUR FAMILY.]

---

26 Traditional words of wisdom during a Xhosa initiation adapted by
NoSomething Ntese for our story's purposes.

Hamba uyokukhulisa usapho, wakhe
nendlu yakho.

[GO RAISE A FAMILY AND BUILD YOUR HOUSE.]

Hamba uyokuthatha ilifa, kunye nendawo
yakho.

[GO TAKE YOUR INHERITANCE AND YOUR RIGHTFUL
POSITION.]

Izinyanya zakho zifuna ubuyele endlwini
kayihlo, uthathe indawo yakho.

[YOUR ANCESTORS WANT YOU TO RETURN TO
YOUR FATHER'S HOUSE AND TAKE YOUR POSITION
THERE.]

Buya ezintabeni, ujongis'umbomb'ekhaya.

[YOU MUST RETURN FROM THE MOUNTAINS TO GO
HOME.]

Zanga iZinyanya zingahamba nawe.

[THE ANCESTORS GO WITH YOU.]

*ORESTES stands and drops his blanket to reveal his
powerful, muscular physique. We see the boy is now a man.
He takes up his new blanket and begins the slow, graceful
'Dance of the Bull'. The* WOMEN *of the* CHORUS *ululate.
They sing rapturously, and encircle him – bumping him (as
tradition dictates) to test his strength. The* WOMEN *of the*
CHORUS *break into stick fighting and ululate as* ORESTES
*slowly makes his way forward and away from the mountain
he has grown up on. They wave to him and resume their
places on their chairs, as Witnesses to the testimonies.*
ORESTES *walks the perimeter of the performance platform.
He has begun the journey of return to his ancestral home.*

ELEKTRA: (*As testimony into the microphone.*)
                 It falls softly: the spirit of revenge.

[27]The brooding Fury finally comes –
leading a child inside the house
to cleanse the stain of blood from long
ago.

KLYTEMNESTRA: (*Testimony.*) I am not so exceeding glad
at the deeds I have done. But we were a
country at war.
It mattered only that we survived.
I had lived so long with the dark figure of
vengeance beneath the bed…
That I suspected nothing the night he
arrived at my door, carrying a tin of ash
and pretending his own death.
We who have done harm to the fathers of
this generation –
We know –
Consequence will arrive –
One dark night –
Unannounced –
At the door.

x: ash

*A series of drum beats signal a knocking at the door of
KLYTEMNESTRA's home.
ELEKTRA appears in a shaft of light, with a kerosene lantern
in her hand. Her mother stands behind her.*

---

27   *The Libation Bearers* (IJ), ll 808, 810–12 [649–51]

ORESTES: (*Shrouded in his blanket.*)
                    Ingaba ngumzi ka Agamemnon lo?
                    [IS THIS THE HOUSE OF AGAMEMNON?]

KLYTEMNESTRA: No Stranger.
                    You are not from these parts or you
                    would know:
                    For many years now – this is the house of
                    Ayesthus and Klytemnestra.

ORESTES: Does Ayesthus, the man of the house,
                    welcome strangers?

KLYTEMNESTRA: (*Suspiciously.*)
                    [28]What country are you from? Who are
                    you?

ORESTES: Announce me to the masters of the
                    house.
                    I've come to bring them news of Orestes.
                    Khawuleza mama! [HURRY UP MAMA.]
                    Night's black chariot is speeding
                    overhead.
                    And it is a long walk home.

KLYTEMNESTRA: We live under the eyes of Justice here.
                    But if your work is serious, men's work,
                    then we must wait for Ayesthus.
                    He is away – but returns late tonight.

Both women turn back to the house.

---

28 Servant in *The Libation Bearers* (IJ), l 819 [657]

ORESTES: I have a message for the mother of
                      Orestes.

They both stop in their tracks and turn back to face the
stranger.

                      Her son is dead.

A strike of the drum. **KLYTEMNESTRA** *gasps in shock.*

ELEKTRA: (*Screams.*) NO!

ORESTES: Here are his ashes –
                      With whom should I leave them?

ELEKTRA, *hearing of the ashes, starts from her grief.*

KLYTEMNESTRA: (*Recovering from her shock to prevent*
                      ELEKTRA *from claiming the ashes.*)
                      I am the mother of Orestes.
                      You may leave them with me.

The **CHORUS** *begins the ephemeral sound of the UMRUHE*
(Mouth Bows) as **KLYTEMNESTRA** *reaches for the ashes.*
She opens the tin and lets her son's supposed remains pour
through her fingers.

                      [29]Now I know – the stock of our ancient
                      masters is perished, root and branch. And
                      the ancient bloodline is blotted out.

ELEKTRA *suddenly lunges for the tin and the two women*
struggle fiercely.

---

29   Adapted from Chorus' words in *Electra* (Sophocles: RCJ) [764–5]

ELEKTRA overpowers her mother, pulling the tin from her.
She falls into ORESTES' arms.
He holds her for a moment. She pushes him and runs.

> Excuse my daughter.
> She is in love with misery.

ORESTES turns to look at her.

> What?
> It must seem strange for me not to grieve
> the death of my only son. [30]But he, who
> sprang from my own life, has been the
> terror of my dreams. Neither by night
> nor day has sweet sleep covered my eyes.
> From moment to moment I have lived
> in the shadow of death. Time's prisoner
> condemned, to wait for my own murder.
> Now this day I am finally rid of the threat
> of him. And her!
> That serpent sucking out my heart's red
> wine.
> Now at last my children are silenced…
> and peace is mine!

ORESTES: I must give this news directly to the man
of the house.

KLYTEMNESTRA: My husband returns after midnight.
But you are welcome to wait here,
Stranger, and eat with us tonight.

---

30   *Electra* (Sophocles: RCJ) [775]

ORESTES:	Ndiyabulela ngempatho yakho entle.
	[THANK YOU FOR YOUR GENEROSITY.]
	I have some business in town – but will
	be back after dark.

KLYTEMNESTRA:	Come when you are ready.
	Tonight – my home is yours.

ORESTES smiles fleetingly and then turns and goes.
KLYTEMNESTRA turns back to the house, but for a
moment feels a presence out in the dark.
She raises her lantern.

Who's there?

*The **CHORUS** of **WOMEN** walk towards the edges of the*
*stage, looking at **KLYTEMNESTRA**.*
The sound of ISITOLO-TOLO (Jew's Harp) accompanies
them.
She turns and retreats into the house.

xi: found

ELEKTRA is lying on her father's grave. She is inconsolable
with grief.

ELEKTRA:	Tata, uOrestes usishiyile!
	[PAPA, ORESTES HAS LEFT US!]
	Ngoluthuthu ndikhalela ilizwe lam.
	[WITH THESE ASHES I CRY FOR MY NATION.]
	Ndikuthanda ngentliziyo yam yonke.
	[I LOVED YOU WITH ALL MY HEART.]

Orestes – you died alone in exile – kude
nekhaya [FAR FROM HOME].
These loving hands could not wash your
corpse, could not help to lift you into the
fire.
Isidumbu sakho sahlanjwa zizandla
ongazaziyo.
[YOUR CORPSE WAS CLEANED AND PREPARED BY
THE HANDS OF STRANGERS.]
Phupho lam, themba lam,
[MY DREAM, MY HOPE,]
Our future is now ash.
Ikamva lethu luthuthu!
[OUR FUTURE IS ASH!]
Ndithathe khon'ukuze ndibe nawe.
[TAKE ME SO THAT I WILL BE WITH YOU.]
Take me as nothing, into your
nothingness, that I may live with you –
Emgodini [IN THE GROUND].
Kuba emhlabeni besimntu mnye,
nasekufeni makube njalo.
[BECAUSE ON EARTH WE WERE ONE, EVEN IN
DEATH LET IT BE SO.]

*She hears someone coming and – fearing it is her mother
– hides behind the* **CHORUS** *of* **WOMEN**, *seated
along the periphery of the earthen floor. The sound of
UMASENGWANA (Milking / Friction Drum) begins.
Entering the cemetery is the stranger who brought* **ELEKTRA**
*the ashes of her brother. Throwing off his blanket, he kneels at
her father's grave. He spits traditional beer in honour of the*

Ancestors, and lights Mphepo (the herb that is burnt when communing with the Ancestors).

ORESTES: Kuwe lizwe lam, nakuni Zinyanya.
                  [TO YOU MY COUNTRY AND TO YOU MY
                  ANCESTORS.]
                  [31]Receive me with good fortune in this
                  journey.
                  Halls of my fathers,
                  Kuba ndize apha ukuza kufezekisa isenzo
                  esibalulekileyo.
                  [I HAVE COME HERE TO FULFIL AN IMPORTANT
                  TASK.]
                  Send me not dishonoured from the land,
                  but grant that I take back what is mine,
                  and restore my house!
                  Ndiyanibongoza, sebenzisanani nam.
                  [PLEASE, WORK WITH ME.]
                  Now I've come back to this land from
                  seventeen years of exile – a man. And I
                  swear on this grave:
                  Ngeke ndibuyele emva ndingakhange
                  ndiziphindisele.
                  [I WILL NOT RETURN WITHOUT MY REVENGE.]

*He turns to go. **ELEKTRA** steps out from the shadows.*

ELEKTRA: (*Breathless.*) Orestes?

He turns to her and they look at each other for a long moment.

---

31   *Electra* (Sophocles: RCJ) [68]

uOrestes?

He nods gently. She steps away from him, afraid. He moves towards her.

Ngeke! [NEVER!] My brother is dead!
You are the one who brought us his ashes!

ORESTES: My sister...dade wethu [MY SISTER] – it is
me.
I still have the stone you gave me as a
child.

ORESTES takes the stone from his pocket. Tentatively she steps towards him and snatches it. She looks at it and falls to her knees.
They embrace for a long moment as she weeps, first in rage and then in joy.

ELEKTRA: Orestes... Orestes...
Let me look at you. Let me look at your
face.
Ungumfanekiso ka yihlo uAgamemnon.
[YOU ARE THE IMAGE OF AGAMEMNON.]
You are your father's son.
[32]Here is Orestes that was dead in craft.
And now by craft restored to life again.
Child of the body that I loved best, at last
you have found me.
You have found those you yearned for.

---

32   *Electra* (Sophocles: SU) [1228–9]

The **CHORUS** *begins the pulse of IGUBU (the Traditional Drum).* **ELEKTRA** *and* **ORESTES** *circle the grave.*

(*Proudly to her brother.*)
Ntsika yesizwe sethu.
[TO YOU THE PILLAR OF THE NATION.]
[33]The seed of hope through all our weeping. Trust your own strength and win back again your father's house.

ORESTES: Zinyanya zakowethu khanyisani indlela.
Ityala eli kweli ngcwaba likhalela impindezelo…
[MY ANCESTORS LIGHT THE WAY. THE CRIME IN THIS GRAVE CRIES OUT FOR JUSTICE]
Let it be done. [34]One murderous stroke is paid off by another lethal blow. So runs the ancient curse, now three generations old.

Two of the **WOMEN** *of the* **CHORUS** *play UMRUBHE (Mouth Bow). The others beat a pulse with their hands on the floor and hum.* **ELEKTRA** *circles the grave, as* **ORESTES** *spits beer over the sacred soil. The following is chanted – building in intensity.*

ELEKTRA: Father that begot us…
[35]Among the dead the savage jaws of fire cannot destroy the spirit.
Father that begot us…

---

33 *The Libation Bearers* (IJ), ll 296–8 [236]

34 Chorus in *The Libation Bearers* (IJ), ll 379–80, 382–3 [312–13, 314]

35 Chorus in *The Libation Bearers* (IJ), ll 393–4 [323–4]

Bawo wethu....sive

[OUR FATHER...HEAR US NOW]

[36]As, in turn, we mourn and weep.

Your two children at your tomb now sing your death song.

[37]Orphans...see us like this both outcasts.

Banished from our home.

Yiba nathi, usincede siphakamise igama lakho.

[BE WITH US AND HELP US TO HONOUR YOUR NAME.]

ORESTES: Father that begot us...

Lord of the world below, see the survivors of our father's line.

Silapha njengeenkedama, singenancedo nakhaya.

[WE ARE HERE AS ORPHANS WITHOUT HELP OR HOME.]

ELEKTRA: Mother that betrayed us...

Isikhohlakali somama

[MOST TERRIBLE MOTHER]

[38]You dared place him in a tomb without the rites of mourning.

ELEKTRA and ORESTES keep moving fluidly around the grave and each other, as the intensity builds.

---

36   The Libation Bearers (IJ), ll 404–6 [332–5]

37   The Libation Bearers (IJ), ll 311, 315–16 [247, 253–4]

38   The Libation Bearers (IJ), ll 533–4 [432–4]

63

[39]You first hacked off his limbs, wazigaxa emqaleni wakhe,

[AND YOU HUNG THEM ON HIS NECK,]

then hung them round his neck. That's how you buried him.

Mother that betrayed us...you made my father's death an abomination.

Wandihlaza [YOU SHAMED ME] and set me apart inside a cell, as if I were some rabid dog.

Ndarhayiza! [I WAILED!] I wept. I died.

She falls into ORESTES' arms and then moves out addressing both the audience and CHORUS.

All who pay attention to this house of trouble hear these words.

Carve them on your heart that we may never forget.

ORESTES: Ungalibali Tata, ungalibali Thongo lam

[DO NOT FORGET FATHER, DO NOT FORGET MY ANCESTOR]

[40]that night that you were slaughtered.

The CHORUS responds with a chanting refrain.

CHORUS: Makubenjalo! [LET IT BE SO!]

ELEKTRA: Ungalibali Tata, ungalibali Thongo lam.

---

39   *The Libation Bearers* [paraphrase] (IJ), ll 540–55 [439–40]

40   *The Libation Bearers* (IJ), l 618 [491]

[DO NOT FORGET FATHER, DO NOT FORGET MY
ANCESTORS.]

[41]The net in which they killed you.

CHORUS: Makubenjalo! [LET IT BE SO!]

ELEKTRA: Ungalibali Tata, ungalibali Thongo lam.
[42]When they covered you with deceit and
shame.

CHORUS: Makubenjalo! [LET IT BE SO!]

ORESTES: Tata sibiza wena.
[FATHER WE ARE CALLING YOU.]
Stand by your children.

ELEKTRA: [43]Through these tears I join his call.
In unison, our voices blend as one – hear
us.
Yiba nathi xa silwayo neentshaba zethu.
[BE WITH US IN FIGHTING OUR ENEMIES.]
Umthetho mawuvelise inyaniso.
[LET JUSTICE REVEAL THE TRUTH.]

CHORUS: Makubenjalo! [LET IT BE SO!]

ORESTES: Father, make me the master of your
house.

---

41   *The Libation Bearers* (IJ), l 619 [492]

42   *The Libation Bearers* (IJ), l 622–3 [494]

43   *The Libation Bearers* (IJ), l 573 [457]

[44]Once drops of blood are shed upon the
ground they cry out for more.

CHORUS: Makubenjalo, kubechosi kube hele!!
                   [LET IT BE SO!]

All instrumentation, humming and rhythms cease.

ELEKTRA: [45]So let the one who bore us grovel.
                   We're bred from her, like wolves, whose
                   savage hearts do not relent.

*A WOMAN of the CHORUS plays the INKINGE (Bow With
Five Litre Tin Can Resonator) and the WOMEN surround
ORESTES and ELEKTRA, as they play at being wolves
together – rolling sensuously in the sand and on one another.*

xii: plan

*KLYTEMNESTRA walks through the WOMEN and crosses
the stage. She mutters to herself, smoking with one hand – a
bottle of whiskey in the other.*

KLYTEMNESTRA: (*To herself.*) [46]I was your chaste and
                   faithful wife; yet I must lose my daughter,
                   while the whore Helen could keep her
                   daughter and live safe and flourishing at
                   home…

---

44   *The Libation Bearers* (IJ), ll 493–4 [400–2]

45   Adapted from *The Libation Bearers* (SU), ll 516–17 [420–2]

46   Clytemnestra to Agamemnon, Euripides, *Iphigenia in Aulis* (SU) [1204]

She stops suddenly – thinking she has heard something. The
CHORUS *ceases their music and foot stamping for a beat.*
She looks around in fear. She moves away. The rhythms
resume.

ORESTES: [47]My plan is simple.
                    I'm expected at our mother's table
                    after dark. Though she knows me as a
                    stranger – we will eat as a family tonight.

ELEKTRA: She will be drunk before the night is out.

ORESTES: I will lay her to bed like a child in the
                    womb…
                    And wait for our stepfather's return.
                    She will see me rip his heart from its cage.
                    And then I will open her in our father's
                    bed.

ELEKTRA: She dreams every night she gives birth to
                    a snake.

ORESTES: [48]I come from the same womb as that
                    snake.
                    This dream fulfils itself in me.
                    She will die by violence for she has
                    nursed a violent thing.

The **CHORUS** *of* **WOMEN** *break into the song ITHONGO*
LAM [MY ANCESTORS LEAD ME].

---

47   *The Libation Bearers* (IJ), l 691 [554]

48   Adapted from *The Libation Bearers* (IJ), l 679 [543]

*ORESTES dances, as ELEKTRA runs home to prepare for
the coming night.*
*The CHORUS move to the table stage right, upon which
KLYTEMNESTRA sits. They lift the table and move it stage
centre with KLYTEMNESTRA borne aloft. A sacrificial
lamb? A drunken Queen in her chariot? The CHORUS
surrounds the table in a half circle, as KLYTEMNESTRA,
behind this human curtain, climbs from the table.*
*The CHORUS move back to their seats dancing and singing
– as ORESTES and KLYTEMNESTRA are seated and
KLYTEMNESTRA lights the candles.*

xiii: home

*All singing stops and in the silence, and we hear the sound of
tearing flesh, as KLYTEMNESTRA divides a roast chicken
and serves herself and ORESTES generous portions.*
*She has been drinking and is clearly inebriated, though still
perfectly in control.*

KLYTEMNESTRA: (*She places a minute potion of food on a
                 plate for ELEKTRA.*) Tata! [TAKE!]

*ELEKTRA is cleaning sodden clothes in a basin nearby. She
takes the food and returns to her seated position on the floor,
to eat. KLYTEMNESTRA notices ORESTES watching this
with emotion.*

                 Let her not move you!
                 She weeps not for the news of her
                 brother!

She grieves the loss of her revenge!

KLYTEMNESTRA tears the chicken's leg.

Something else to eat?

ORESTES: Ndiyabulela mama! [THANK YOU MA!]

KLYTEMNESTRA: (*Hissing at ELEKTRA.*)
Hang it up to dry!

ELEKTRA pulls from the bowl of washing, an enormous
male labourer's uniform. She hangs it on a hook. It conjures
the shape of its owner: Ayesthus. The sheer size of it indicates
the intimidating and enormous physical presence he holds
in the house. His boots – equally gargantuan – wait beside
ELEKTRA, to be polished.

My husband went to see his mother for
month end.
But stay as late as you need. Ayesthus will
be pleased to meet the man who brought
home the ashes of my son.

BOOTS!

ELEKTRA removes her boots for her. KLYTEMNESTRA
suddenly grabs ELEKTRA by the arm.

Speak all that is in your heart, and tell me
that your father's death was not deserved.

She releases ELEKTRA from her grip and lights a cigarette,
lost in her drunken thoughts.

ELEKTRA and ORESTES exchange glances. ELEKTRA
places her mother's boots beside the boots of Ayesthus, and
begins to polish.

	How many children can a mother lose?
	First it was my baby he smashed against a rock.
	Then Ephigenia – sacrificed like a goat.
	And now Orestes – gone!
ORESTES:	I have heard this story in the village.
	Wenza ntoni wena ke mama? [WHAT DID YOU DO MA? ('MA' AS A MEANS OF ADDRESSING AN OLDER WOMAN WITH RESPECT, RATHER THAN LITERALLY 'MOTHER'.)]
	How did you take your revenge?
KLYTEMNESTRA:	I took a lover…

Pointing to the suspended uniform.

Ayesthus! [49] And planned to welcome
my husband home – not with crown or
garland…
but with a sharpened axe.

KLYTEMNESTRA stands, to re-enact the scene.

[50] When my conquering husband
returned…

---

49   Electra in *Electra* (Sophocles: SU) [163–4]

50   Source unknown

We lit fires throughout the city, feigning celebrations. Crimson tapestries were laid between Agamemnon and the entrance of our home.
And reaching towards him I whispered for the whole city to hear:
'Come to me now my love, down from the car of war, but step upon these tapestries we have lain to honour your coming home. Those feet that have stamped out our enemies need never touch earth again, my great one.'

She picks up the enormous boots and walks them along the edge of the table, conjuring Agamemnon's last steps.

And they never did.
(*Simply.*) We killed him dead.

She throws the boots to the ground to the thump of IGUBU (the Drum).

That was the last night I saw my boy – Orestes.
Seventeen years I had not seen him.
And now…never more.

KLYTEMNESTRA takes a small pair of shoes from her pocket that once belonged to ORESTES. A WOMAN of the CHORUS sings softly. KLYTEMNESTRA begins to cry. ORESTES is visibly moved.

[51]Girl – It was ever your nature to love
your father…
But sons have a deeper affection for their
mothers…
And mothers for their sons.
As a babe – I could not wean him from
the breast.
He was just a little boy when she took
him away.
(*Addressing the shoes.*) Orestes…
I never saw you a man.

ELEKTRA:　　　(*Sensing **ORESTES'** sudden emotion, steps
between them.*)
She has no right to use my brother's
name.

KLYTEMNESTRA:　　(*In **ELEKTRA**'s ear, with renewed cruelty.*)
Ayesthus and I danced in your father's
blood…

*KLYTEMNESTRA takes the arms of the hanging uniform
and dances, as a **WOMAN** from the **CHORUS** plays a jaunty
tune on IFLEYITI (Harmonica).
Returning to **ELEKTRA**, she stands inches from her.*

We revealed your father's broken body for
all to see.
'Here lies Agamemnon, my husband,
made a corpse by this right hand – a
masterpiece of Justice. Done is done.'

51　Adapted from *Electra* (Euripides: EPC) [1102–3]

She sits heavily, unable to support herself. She is now terribly drunk.

                    (*Slurring.*) Done is done! Done is done…

The playing of IFLEYITI (Harmonica) resumes, as KLYTEMNESTRA sways to the music and then passes out cold. Three WOMEN from the CHORUS step forward. One stands behind KLYTEMNESTRA and begins to play ISITOLO-TOLO (Jew's Harp). The two other WOMEN of the CHORUS come around the table to look at KLYTEMNESTRA. They chuckle between themselves. ELEKTRA removes the cigarette from her mother's hand. KLYTEMNESTRA starts awake to find ORESTES standing over her. He holds out his arms and she obliges like a child. He lifts her in his arms and makes to carry her to her bed – but not before she leans back to snatch her whiskey bottle from the table. He lays her on her Testimony Table, where the WOMEN of the CHORUS wait. ELEKTRA climbs onto the table with the axe in her hand for the first time.

ELEKTRA: [52]If you prick us – do we not bleed?
                          If you tickle us – do we not laugh?
                          If you poison us – do we not die?
                          And if you wrong us…
                          Shall we not revenge?

ORESTES returns to the table. ELEKTRA pulls him towards her.

---

52   *The Merchant of Venice* by William Shakespeare, III.i, ll 49–61

If you go now – you will find Ayesthus
crossing the field towards the house.
Slaughter him like a beast and bring me
his heart.

ORESTES: Father that begot us…
Lord of the world below, see the survivors
of our father's line.
Silapha njengeenkedama singenancedo
nakhaya.
[WE ARE HERE AS ORPHANS WITHOUT HELP OR
HOME.]

ELEKTRA: [53]As there is justice in Heaven.

IGUBU (A drum beat) from the **CHORUS**.
ELEKTRA and **ORESTES** climb onto the table and stand
with arms spread to the Heavens.

And fire in the hands of the gods.
Our reckoning must be made.
Umhlaba mawuxelele abaphantsi ukuba
siyeza.
[THE EARTH SHOULD TELL OUR ANCESTORS THAT
WE ARE COMING.]
Here we come.
The tide is turning at last.

*ORESTES jumps from the table and, with weapon in
hand, sets out for the field to find Ayesthus. The actor walks
the full periphery of the stage, in a stylized, protracted*

---

53   Source unknown

manner. The **WOMEN** *of the* **CHORUS***, smoking their pipes,*
watch him go.

xiv: curse

ELEKTRA moves to the uniform of Ayesthus. She removes
it from its hook, throws it to the ground and spits on it.
KLYTEMNESTRA starts awake. ELEKTRA disappears
beneath the table.

KLYTEMNESTRA: *(Suddenly up with a stick in her hand.)*
        Who's there?

She is off the bed and moving towards the 'kitchen' again.
A **WOMAN** *of the* **CHORUS** *is softly Beat Dancing*
– creating a rhythm with her feet. She stands beside
KLYTEMNESTRA, who cannot see her. KLYTEMNESTRA
notices the uniform on the ground.

        Ayesthus – are you home?

With her back turned, **ELEKTRA** *hangs a large dead snake*
behind **KLYTEMNESTRA** *and slips back beneath the table.*
KLYTEMNESTRA turns to see the snake and screams. The
CHORUS WOMAN *intensifies the rhythmic movement*
of her feet. IGUBU (the Traditional Drum) assumes the
quickening of the rhythm, like a heartbeat that is racing.
KLYTEMNESTRA lights Mphepho (herb that is burnt when
communing with the Ancestors).
She smothers the dead animal in the smoke – in an attempt
to neutralise the curse that has been put on her House.

Hamba Moyomube! Hamba Satan!

[AWAY EVIL SPIRITS! AWAY SATAN!]

She stands with stick in hand and calls out.

I am from the house of Atreus!
I fear none!

The **WOMEN** *of the* **CHORUS** *move into the space, singing.*
They clear all set elements.

xv: vengeance

Out in the field, **ORESTES** *breaks into a run. As the*
CHORUS *sings,* **ORESTES'** *feet lift from the ground.*
Suspended (by stage device) he continues his long strides
towards his destiny. He lifts the pickaxe and swings it above
his head. His body is carried by the weight of the weapon, in
fluid circular motions – until he strikes violently at Ayesthus'
boots centre stage. The boots, filled with blood, spill their
contents across the stage. **ORESTES** *tears a large heart*
from one of the boots and stumbles backwards. One of the
WOMEN *of the* **CHORUS**, *who raised him, appears to him.*
He is unsure if she is real or a vision. He drops to his knees
stunned.

Ma **NOSOMETHING:** Mntwan'am! Kutheni ubulala nje?

[MY CHILD! WHY DO YOU KILL?]

Umntu akabulawa.

[A HUMAN BEING SHOULD NEVER BE MURDERED.]

Uyalazi ukuba igazi lomntu liya
kukumangalela?

[DO YOU KNOW THAT HUMAN BLOOD WILL HAUNT
YOU ALWAYS?]

Imbi lento uyenzayo.

[WHAT YOU HAVE DONE IS TERRIBLE]

Ungaze uphinde ubulale. [NEVER KILL AGAIN.]

ORESTES reaches for her but she is gone.

xvi: lost

ELEKTRA: Orestes…? Orestes…?

*ELEKTRA is crawling through the field, looking for her
brother.*

ORESTES: Ndikuphathele yonke into owake
                      wayifuna…

                      [I HAVE BROUGHT YOU ALL THAT YOU EVER
                      WANTED…]

*He lifts the heart towards her. She takes it from him and
starts to laugh and then weep. She puts Ayesthus' boots on
and dances wildly.*

ELEKTRA: At last – Ayesthus, you are what you
                      always were…
                      an animal without a heart.
                      And now s'thandwa sami [DARLING] – for
                      the greater deed.
                      She is asleep in our father's bed.
                      Open her tonight and finally set us free.

ORESTES: Elektra – we are lost!

ELEKTRA: (*Stunned for a moment, but recovering instantly.*)
Famous spirit of Revenge – you have done your ancestors proud!
Ungalibali Tata, ungalibali Thongo lam!
[DO NOT FORGET MY FATHER, DO NOT FORGET MY ANCESTOR!]

ORESTES: That night that he was slaughtered.

ELEKTRA: Ungalibali Tata, ungalibali Thongo lam.
[DO NOT FORGET MY FATHER, DO NOT FORGET MY ANCESTOR!]
How they covered you with deceit and shame.

ORESTES: Tata sibiza wena.
[FATHER WE ARE CALLING YOU]
Stand by your children.
[54]By the gods – by my own hand,
Let me kill my mother – then let me die.

xvii: truth

*There is a strike of the drum. **ELEKTRA** and **ORESTES** turn to find **KLYTEMNESTRA** standing behind them. She is staring wildly at **ORESTES**.*

---

54   Source unknown

KLYTEMNESTRA: Of course – the dark face of Agamemnon.
My son, my child, Orestes – raised from
the dead.
At last in the flesh.
Not the stranger with the ashes – or the
shadow over my bed…but a man before
me, carrying the face of my darkest
nights.

ELEKTRA: The man you spread your legs for in my
father's bed…
Nantsi intliziyo yakhe –
[HERE IS HIS HEART]
You have his heart…

She places the heart at her mother's feet.

Thatha! [HERE!]
Do with it as you will!

KLYTEMNESTRA: (*Screams in agony, falling to her knees.*)
NO!
[55]My love, my power…
Dead.

ELEKTRA: [56]By whose side you soon will lie as a
corpse and you shall be his bride in Hell's
halls as wife you were to him on earth.

KLYTEMNESTRA: You stupid girl, you witless child –
You know not what you do.

---

55   Adapted from *The Libation Bearers* (IJ), l 1110 [893]

56   Adapted from *Electra* (Euripides: EPC) [1144–5]

Already the darkness is in your eyes.

You become me. You choose the curse.

ELEKTRA circles KLYTEMNESTRA dangerously.

ELEKTRA: Ndikhetha isiqalekiso?

[I CHOOSE THE CURSE?]

You were my ruin – ndingazange

ndakwenza nto imbi.

[THOUGH I DID NOTHING TO HARM YOU.]

You poisoned me with your deeds.

You are the shadow that fell on my life

and made a child of me through fear.

I have hated you so long and now...

YOU WANT TO LOOK INTO MY

HEART? SIES!

ELEKTRA and ORESTES circle KLYTEMNESTRA.

A WOMAN from the CHORUS begins UMNGQOKOLO

(Split-Tone Singing).

KLYTEMNESTRA: (*To herself.*)

[57]It comes upon me as prophesied.

I was the two-footed lioness that bore

these wanting wolves.

I killed – and now must die.

But not without a fight will the destroyer

be destroyed.

[58]BRING ME MY MAN-KILLING AXE!

---

57   Adapted from Cassandra in *Agamemnon* (SU) [1256, 1258]

58   Adapted from *The Libation Bearers* (SU) [1889]

*The **CHORUS** joins the UMNGQOKOLO (Split-Tone Singing).*

KLYTEMNESTRA is suddenly up and racing towards the pick-axe lying on the ground. ORESTES and ELEKTRA close in. ELEKTRA snatches the axe before she can reach it. ORESTES grabs a flailing KLYTEMNESTRA, pulling her to the ground. She cannot move.

	(*Pleading.*)
	[59]My son, – hear me – For I will say this only once.
	Upon this breast you often lay asleep.
	And from here you sucked the milk that made you strong.
	I gave you life. And if you take mine – you will never know peace again.
ELEKTRA:	(*Circling her mother and brother, axe in hand.*)
	This night's end is already written.
	Our destiny must be played out!
KLYTEMNESTRA:	Nothing…nothing is written.
	Do not choose to be me. [60]The hounds that avenge all murder will forever hunt you down.
ELEKTRA:	This is the son of Agammemnon.
	His hour is come at last.

---

59   Adapted from *The Libation Bearers* (IJ), ll 1115–16 [896–8]

60   Adapted from *The Libation Bearers* (IJ), ll 1147–8 [924]

ORESTES: (*In rage and pain.*)
YOU HAVE MADE ME WHAT I AM!!

KLYTEMNESTRA: (*Lowering her head, ready for the blow
from the axe.*)
Then strike my child – and be done.

xviii: shift

*ORESTES lifts the axe high over his head, but as he prepares
to kill his mother, a **WOMAN** from the **CHORUS** starts to
sing a haunting song. **ORESTES** tries to shake off the sound
of it.*

ELEKTRA: Yini? [WHAT?] Why do you pause?

*He lifts the axe again, but the **WOMEN** rise and move across
the performance area. He tries several times to see the deed
through – but cannot.*

ORESTES: NeZinyanya ziyayazi lo nto…
[EVEN THE ANCESTORS KNOW THIS…]

Throwing down the axe.

I cannot shed more blood.

ELEKTRA: But the Furies demand it. They cry out
for more.

ORESTES: (*Grabbing her.*) There is still time, Sister.
Walk away.

Rewrite this ancient end.

ELEKTRA: (*Wrenching herself loose.*)
Don't ask me to forget my hatred! There
can be no forgiveness!
Slay her like the animal she is.

ORESTES: I am tired of hating.

ELEKTRA: Go then and keep company where you
belong…
Na bafazi! [WITH WOMEN!]
I will do this thing on my own.

ORESTES: WHAT IS IT YOU WANT?

ELEKTRA: (*She screams from her soul.*)
VENGEANCE!
An eye for an eye and a tooth for a tooth!

ORESTES: That was the curse of our Mother's House.
I have been there tonight and it's empty.
It's a circle with no end.

ELEKTRA: My father's blood will be paid back here
tonight.
I am from the House of Atreus. I will do
what must be done.

*She grabs the axe and runs at **KLYTEMNESTRA** screaming.*

xix: rises

The WOMEN of the CHORUS move swiftly as one. They
grab ELEKTRA and overpower her.
ELEKTRA screams in rage as they wrestle the axe from
her hands. They restrain her and she finally breaks down
and weeps for all the injustices done to her, her brother and
her father. She slowly finds her breath. UMASENGWANA
(Milking / Friction Drum) begins its deep, haunting sound.
ELEKTRA emerges from the knot of WOMEN. She and
ORESTES are focused on their mother – still cowering centre
stage. They crawl towards her slowly. KLYTEMNESTRA
– uncertain of what they will do to her – draws back in terror.
As they reach their mother, they slowly stand together and
extend their hands to help her up. Once on her feet, she is a
broken woman. She backs away and leaves the performance
platform, resuming her place at her Testimony Table.
The WOMEN of the CHORUS explode into song, circling
brother and sister. ELEKTRA and ORESTES embrace,
weeping. They have triumphed over their destiny of
vengeance.
The cycle has been broken.
The Diviner of the group steps forward. She prays, as the
others chant in response.

> [61]Ndinqula aMambathane
>
> [I PRAISE THE MBATHANES]
>
> OoMatshaya, ooXesibe
>
> [I PRAISE THE MATSHAYAS, THE XESIBES]
>
> Ndinqula uBhomoyi [I PRAISE BHOMOYI]

---

61 The below praises are from Nofenishala Mvotyo. They include the names
of her Ancestors, as well as her prayer for South Africa. The content of this
praise / prayer varies at each performance.

USophitsho, uNgqolomsila
[SOPHITSHO, NGQOLOMSILA]

UYemyem [YEMYEM]

Ndinqula uGcaleka, uTshilo
[I PRAISE GCALEKA, TSHILO]

Mthi wembotyi [MTHI WEMBOTYI]

Nditsho kumama ke Xa nditshoyo…
[I'M TALKING TO MY MOTHER IN PARTICULAR,
WHEN I SAY THAT…]

Ndiqulela umanyano lwabantu
Abamhlophe nabantsundu
[I PRAY FOR UNITY BETWEEN BLACK AND WHITE]

Sinqulela abantwana bethu
[WE PRAY FOR OUR CHILDREN]

Bayeke ubundlobongela nokubulalana
[THAT THEY MAY STOP CRIME AND KILLING EACH
OTHER]

Sicela umsebenzi lo siwenzayo
[WE ASK THAT THE WORK THAT WE ARE DOING]

Siwenze ngempumelelo – sibenamandla
[MAY WE DO IT WITH SUCCESS – AND POWER]

Sithethe inyaniso.
[AND SPEAK THE TRUTH.]

epilogue

*The **CHORUS**, **ELEKTRA** and **ORESTES** stand facing the
audience.*
*KLYTEMNESTRA is at her Testimony Table. She speaks into
the microphone.*

KLYTEMNESTRA: It falls softly the residue of revenge...
Like rain.
And we who made the sons and
daughters of this land, servants in the
halls of their forefathers...
We know.
We are still only here by grace alone.
[62]Look now – dawn is coming.
Great chains on the home are falling off.
This house rises up.
For too long it has lain in ash on the
ground.

The full company stands in silence looking out at the audience.
A fine powdery substance gently floats down on them –

As lights fade to black.

---

62   Adapted from *The Libation Bearers* (IJ), l 1199 [961]

RAM
THE ABDUCTION OF SITA INTO DARKNESS

ORIGINALLY COMMISSIONED BY

THE CULTURE PROJECT

Artistic Director, Allan Buchman

Special Thanks

This adaptation was inspired by *Ramesh Menon's* magnificent prose retelling of *The Ramayana*. My profound gratitude for his opening the gates to the rest of us.

R.K Narayan & Ranchor Prime's short prose versions were also helpful. My thanks goes to the above and any other writers who may have impacted upon me while creating this text.

The ending I have chosen for this version of *The Ramayana* is inspired by an ancient Southern Indian tale and is recounted by Ramesh Menon in the final pages of his *Ramayana* retelling.

Allan Buchman – for choosing me to adapt this wonder.

Lekha Singh – for initiating & enabling this adventure.

Anant Jesse – for a rainy afternoon of black chocolate, orange juice and rama revelations in the garden.

Brian Drader – for your continued generosity, insights and exquisite gift for the lazer-precise questions that lead a writer to their own answers.

RAM

The abduction of Sita into darkness

"In the summer of 1988, sanitation workers across North India went on strike.[1]

Their demand was simple: They wanted the federal government to sponsor more episodes of a television serial based on the Indian epic Ramayana. The serial, which had been running on India's state-owned television channel for more than a year, had proved to be an extraordinarily popular phenomenon, with more than eighty million Indians tuning in to every weekly episode. Streets in all towns and cities emptied on Sunday mornings as the serial went on the air. In villages with no electricity, people usually gathered around a rented TV set powered by a car battery. Many bathed ritually and garlanded their television sets before settling down to watch Rama, the embodiment of righteousness, triumph over adversity. When the government, faced with rising garbage mounds and a growing risk of epidemics, finally relented and commissioned more episodes of The Ramayana, not just the sanitation workers but millions of Indians celebrated."

1 Pankaj Mishra in his Introduction to R.K Narayan's *The Ramayana*

Characters

VALMIKI SAMAJ[2]
Sanitation Workers, Keepers of the Sita-Body

RAMA
Ordained King of Ayodhya

SITA
Beloved of Rama

SITA - BODY
Body of Sita

LAKSHMANA
Brother of Rama

DASARATHA
Father of Rama

RAVANA
King of Sri Lanka

KAUSALYA
Mother of Rama

MANDODARI
Wife of Ravana

2 The word "bhangi" (sweeper) denotes an Indian caste. "Bhangis" are
treated as "untouchables" and typically belong to the "Valmiki Samaj" (a
sanskritised and perhaps more sanitized name than "bhangi"). "Valmiki
Samaj" are traditionally restricted to the sanitation work of cleaning
latrines and handling dead bodies (both human and animal). There
are a number of disparate communities, tribals, and nomadic groups
from different parts of India, who call themselves 'valmikis', claiming
to be descendants of Maharishi Valmiki, the first known author of the
'Ramayana'. (Susan Abraham's "A Sanitation Worker's Mumbai Dreams")

INDRAJIT
Son of Ravana

VIBHEESHANA
Brother of Ravana

SUGRIVA
Monkey King

VALI
Brother to Sugriva

HANUMAN
Monkey God Devotee of Rama

KUSHA AND LAVA
Street Urchin Sons of Rama

+ varuna; goddess of the sea
Incarnated by performer of the SITA-BODY

+ jatavu; ancient eagle warrior
Incarnated and / vocalized by performer of DASARATHA

+ garuda: half man half bird
Incarnated and / vocalized by performer of DASARATHA

+ the golden deer
Incarnated and / vocalized by performer of RAVANA

+the valmiki samaj
The valmiki samaj may be performed (as described in this text)
by the performers of KAUSALYA and MANDODARI. As with
all the additional characters above, performers doubling on roles
is optional.

Mise-En-Scene

The ideal performance space for RAM is a high-ceilinged urban-industrial room of stark, worn beauty. Seating is steeply raked to look down on and "hold" the performance on three sides or in the round. (Proscenium arch with a raised stage would be anathema to this work). The high ceilinged walls are covered in plastic-wrapped scaffolding, as though undergoing construction. The movement of the plastic sheets from the "wind" of large industrial fans, creates an unsettling, haunting sound. Before entering the performance area the audience is invited to remove their shoes and place them in a pile. Strewn around the performance area are piles of debris and tethered plastic bags – a bleak yet ethereal landscape of urban waste. Centre of the performance area is a large, ungainly television (circa 1970s) powered by a car battery and garlanded with dead flowers. The television screen is filled with the "searching" pattern of snowy static: the void we recognize when a television is sitting between channels. Static sonics fill the auditorium with its soft but disturbing sound.

The snow pattern of the television is reflected on the back wall of the space – creating epic presence from the banal domestic. Placed before the old television is a stunningly worn, long sofa. Seated in this sofa, standing behind and around it – is the full company [with the exception of the SITA-BODY, hidden beneath the waste of the landscape].

Prologue

As lights fade, the cast slowly rise from the sofa and drift away. The television is unplugged from the car battery by the last remaining members of the company and removed. Finally it is only the VALMIKI SAMAJ who remain. They sift through the layers of tethered plastic bags and waste, with a singular and unhurried air. Finally VALMIKI SAMAJ signals to the other. At her feet, curled in a fetal position and wrapped in plastic, is the body of a woman. She is handsome, naked and dead. The VALMIKIS cover their mouths with fabric, tear the plastic open and unwrap the broken SITA-BODY. They sing softly of death.

A woman rises from where she was concealed beneath the SITA BODY. Life force separates from its physical form. She stands beside the dead SITA BODY, but remains invisible to the VALMIKI SAMAJ. She is SITA.

SITA:
> Do not grieve for me. I am glad to go.
> Freer than you are, still in the body of pain.
>
> *(Regarding the SITA-BODY)*
>
> This Body made only for sorrow.
> Burn after reading – but first read it well.
> There on the skin, in the bones, beneath the feet worn for this life
> Trace the journeys and dreams it once lived.
>
> *(One of the VALMIKIS tending to the corpse, speaks quietly)*

VALMIKI 1: She was born – like she died – in a furrow of earth. Janaka found her in a field early one dawn, at the head of his plough. A few hours old, almost dead from the cold – he lifted her into his arms, named the foundling Sita, took her home and raised her as his own. Sita… Bearer of Great Sorrows. Wife to Rama in this lifetime. Lying naked in the dark folds of the Great Mother's skirt at birth – and now in death too – waiting once again to be taken home.

> *(Singing, the VALMIKI SAMAJ unfold the SITA-BODY from its fetal position and uncover two newborn infants – blue and suckling at her cold breasts)*

VALMIKI 2: At the close of her life – she used the last she had, to tear the sons of Rama from her body, into this broken world.

(The VALMI SAMAJ lift the newborn boys from the SITA BODY and move away to her left and right. The umbilical chords remain attached growing longer as the VALMIKI SAMAJ move)

VALMIKI 1: At the world's edge, the boys grew like orphaned buds in the wild. They spoke only in song. They sang only the story of their birthright: The Ishvaku Legacy carved forever on the tongues of Sita and Rama's sons.

(The VALMIKIS cut the umbilical chords. The babies scream. Their cries show the years that lapse, becoming the beautiful and haunting song of two street urchins KUSA and LAVA: RAMA's lost sons. Theirs is an ancient, dissonant sound – filled with beauty and grief. SITA stands amidst the urban detritus, dust and fluttering plastic bags)

SITA: But let us not speak yet of loss, my beloved.
Let us sing rather of the beginning… When you first travelled beyond Ayhoda's walls. I found you at dusk – washing blood from your hands in the river outside my city. We were – neither of us – yet 16 summers old.

1: Essence

(RAMA is kneeling at the water, cleaning his hands. He looks up to find SITA watching him)

RAMA: Blood.

    (She just looks at him)

    It gets in the nails…

    (He looks away)

SITA: Whose blood is it on your hands?

    (RAMA looks at her sharply)

RAMA: Those with blood on theirs.

SITA: Did their deaths heal what they harmed?

RAMA: No. *(Jaw clenched)* But they will not harm again.

SITA: Then why, my lord, are you so sad?

    (RAMA is quiet, he looks up to search her face)

RAMA: Where I'm from, life grows steadily, inevitably as trees. No one dies in Ayhoda who is not yet old.

SITA: Peaceful Ayhoda is all you have known?

RAMA: *(Nodding)* It is my first time beyond the gates. I have seen things since that cannot be put into words. Mothers, children – used and buried, though not yet dead. The ground was still moving when we found them. All we could do… *(He cannot go on)*

SITA: *(Nodding)* The work of Ravana of Lanka's legions.

RAMA: *(Grimly)* Blood does not wash easily, but I am happy for these stains.
I feel – perhaps for the first time – awake.

SITA: *(Smiling gently)* Or have you just fallen into the slumber of duality from which few of us ever wake?

(RAMA nods, understanding her. The VALMIKI exhale. RAMA puts his head down, overcome with grief. He covers his face. SITA goes to him, takes his hands, washes them, kisses each finger and then gently kisses each eye – including the third)

SITA: *(Indicating her city over her shoulder)* In Mathila too, they believe the world ends at the city gate. It is my daily practice since I was a child – to rise before dawn, and crawl the tunnel I made under the wall. I wake in a fever every morning and must wander into the wild – to see the truth for myself.

RAMA: Out here alone? What does your father say?

SITA: He does not know.

(He looks at her for a long moment)

RAMA: Who are you, soul?

SITA: *(Smiling)* No one knows to whom I was borne.
But I am the foundling of Janaka of Mathila. They call me Sita in this lifetime, my Lord.

RAMA: Are you promised?

SITA: Only to the mortal man who can string Siva's bow. *(She laughs gently at the absurdity of this)* And so I am promised to no one at all!

(She smiles. He does not)

RAMA: Show me this bow.

II.

(VALMIKI 1 moves around the SITA-BODY, singing of marriage. She begins to paint the naked flesh with intricate henna markings. VALMIKI 2 wraps SITA in the sari of a bride)

SITA: Let us not sing yet of loss. Let us sing of how you found me, as you have in every lifetime… And once again brought me home.

(RAMA lays himself over the SITA-BODY, now animated with life, and pulls it into the embrace of their first wedding night. SITA watches from nearby)

VALMIKI 2: The opening to the female body is but a portal to the great mystery of entering the fires of this realm; A gateway only accessible through Her form. The inevitable longing to possess her, is dark ego rising. That first longing for what can never truly be owned... Is the start of the sacred fall.

(She turns the SITA-BODY over, wipes the blood from between her legs and resumes painting her body. VALMIKI 1 removes the fabric covering her face and assumes the role of KAUSALYA – RAMA's mother. She gathers the naked, sleeping RAMA in her arms like a child)

KAUSALYA: Much is written of a mother's love. What more need be said of the 9 moons I carried the blue one in my waters, before he passed through the static and into this world?

Childless in middle age, my husband performed a yagna begging that one of his three wives be blessed with a son.

(Lights rise on DASARATHA, with arms outstretched. He lets handfuls of dry, dusty rice pour between his fingers and scatter, smoking on the floor)

The Gods answered with not one son from us – but four.

(The pipes of the scaffolding drip and form pools. The scaffolding's plastic coverings tremor and billow)

History tells that when I bore Rama late into the night – I made no sound for "there was no pain". But his story too, was written by men. Too well I recall the white heat, as my body tore open. A woman can smile as she is drowning, no? *(A shower of petals from the skies)* The future of Yuvaraja passed between my legs, as Rama – Dasaratha's first and most beloved son – was born.

III.

(DASARATHA, a powerful and aging man, holds KAUSALYA in a sensuous embrace. Her long dark hair hangs over her naked back)

DASARATHA: *(Confiding in her)* They say I love him too much.

KAUSALYA: Loving a child is constant preparation in grief.

DASARATHA: Do I love our son too much? What do you say?

KAUSALYA: Everything is Brahman, my Lord. Love him more
– love him less. Someday, he too will be gone. *(To audience)*
Many years ago – my hair was still black… And my opinion
still asked for.

VALMIKI 2: Many years ago – our hair was once black…
And our opinions still asked for.

*(VALMIKI 2 holds KAUSALYA's hair at the roots and pulls her fingers
through it leaving the hair streaked with white. DASARATHA disappears
from behind her, leaving her alone. She slips her robe over her shoulders
and covers herself)*

KAUSALYA: Younger wives must have their time. What losses can
we speak of as our beauty fades? And each day makes us a
little more invisible still.

(VALMIKI 2 continues pulling white through KAUSALYA's hair)

When Rama returned with beautiful Sita, his bride – I found
reason again to dress and face the world. But ask any first wife:
The waiting never leaves your soul.

*(SITA stands behind KAUSALYA, and brushes her long graying hair.
SITA's own black hair is striking in contrast)*

SITA: Tomorrow: Mother to a King.

(She sees KAUSALYA's stunned face)

You did not know?

KAUSALYA: *(Embarrassed)* It is many years since Dasaratha took
my counsel. *(Gathering herself)* It is his Dharma. Rama now
belongs to his people.

SITA: Everyday, he will be less mine. How will I bear it. Ma?

KAUSALYA: Men cannot know grief until it sits at their table. We
smell its shadow as children. We know its depth in the long
nights of giving birth. In the agony of those hours, we brush
shoulders with what waits for us all. Men know loss as death

on the battlefield. We hear its song at the turning of each new moon.

SITA: *(Eyes tearing)* Perhaps I am yet a child but without Rama I know I would die. As a shadow cannot be without its substance – I would simply cease to be.

KAUSALYA: The surrendering is the free-falling that we master, my dear. A smiling baby plunges from our arms and does not shatter its spine.

SITA: *(Brushing tears away, smiling)* Tell me again of when he was born.

KAUSALYA: *(Combing SITA's dark hair)* Rama came to us as dark as the forest... blue black. Lakshmana-born to Dasaratha's second wife – was pale and haunting as the moon. Two halves of the same lunar light. As children, they would sit for weeks watching the monsoons together – Lakshmana at Rama's knee. It has always been Lakshmana's dharma to protect his brother. Better yet... for what is to come...

SITA: Ma, why do you speak of loss on the eve of Yuvaraja? Tomorrow Rama will be King.

KAUSALYA: I am old, Sita. The future shows itself to me around the edges of the nights. I feel a tide moving in... And our heart will surely be born away when it draws back at dawn.

IV.

(KAUSALYA is braiding SITA's hair as they talk. RAMA has been watching them for awhile since he entered the room. LAKSHMANA waits behind him. RAMA's mother sees him and rises. He prostrates himself at her feet)

KAUSALYA: Rise – King of all Tomorrows.

(He stands and she takes his hands)

You're trembling.

RAMA: *(Not looking her in the eye)* I've come to say goodbye.

(RAMA does not look at SITA but keeps his gaze steadily on his mother, who is silent for awhile)

Our father is indebted to our fourth mother from many years ago. Tonight she has asked that he give her what she demands.

KAUSALYA: *(Beginning to understand the gravity)* Shantam Paapam! Evil be still!

SITA: *(Barely able to breathe)* What does he owe her?

KAUSALYA: *(Nodding, unable to look up)* His life.

(They all look to KAUSALYA who moves to the fire)

When Rama's father met Kaiyiki, she fast became his favourite and traveled with him... even to the battlefields during times of war. One night, as he lay dying from his wounds – beyond a woman's strength – she gathered him up and walked out of the encampment with him in her girl arms. He promised her any two wishes for saving his life. I see tonight – on the eve of your coronation – she has come calling on his unbreakable word.

SITA: What has she asked?

RAMA: *(Unable to look at SITA)*
I will leave Ayhoda, before dawn, for fourteen years exile in the wild.

(SITA is stunned. KAUSALYA nods slowly, horrified but in recognition of her earlier unease) And in my absence, Dasaratha will crown her own born son, Yuvaraja, in my place.

KAUSALYA: *(Understanding all)* At last – Mother to a King.

RAMA: I don't have much time. I must leave before the city wakes.

(SITA looks wildly to LAKSHMANA who stands silently nearby)

SITA: And Dasaratha agreed to this?

(LAKSHMANA nods, jaw clenched. SITA is breathless)

Without his son, Dasaratha will die. Why would he blindly do as Kaikiki's ambition demands?

KAUSALYA: *(Quietly, looking at RAMA and LAKSHMANA)* Because, my dear, the men of the Ishvaku House will honour a promise above all else.

RAMA: Leaving is my Dharma. *(Straining against the emotion)* I am blessed to follow where it leads me.

LAKSHMANA: *(Unable to contain his disgust and rage)* A King surely thinks what is best for his people, and not what suits his favourite whore!

KAUSALYA: No more, Lakshmana! I love Rama as you do. But that "whore" is one of four mothers to you both.

LAKSHMANA: As God is my witness, someday I will repay her. And the world will forgive me my sin.

RAMA: Kaiyiki is but an instrument of dharma, brother.

LAKSHMANA: *(Eyes filling with tears of rage)* Not my mother by blood but mother all the same… I have loved her since I was a boy. But I will never forgive her this, Rama.

RAMA: Brother, we have sat side by side at our master's feet and learned dharma…

LAKSHMANA: And I must honour mine: To protect you always and from all things. Even a mother.

RAMA: The soul's path is eternal. What is fourteen years in the wild?

LAKSHMANA: Listen to me Rama. No one, not the Devas nor Kings would stand against your becoming King today. By violence, if needs be.

RAMA: *(Taking him squarely by the shoulders, looking into his eyes)* Think with your cool head - not the fire in your heart. The Ishvaku men do not break their word.

(Turning to KAUSALYA) Give me your blessing, please. *(Straining)* At least let me go in some peace.

(KAUSALYA looks at RAMA intensely for a long moment)

KAUSALYA: *(Quietly but resolved)* Narayana give me strength every moment of these fourteen years ahead. I will be waiting for you, Rama. Go now, with my prayers.

(He lays himself at her feet. She lays her hand on his head. RAMA rises and turns to LAKSHMANA)

LAKSHMANA: Nothing you say will matter. I go where you go.

RAMA: *(Smiles)* I know better than to try. Go. Gather what we need and no more.

(They embrace. LAKSHMANA goes to KAUSALYA for her blessing, embraces her tenderly and leaves to prepare. For the first time since he entered the room – RAMA turns to SITA, with his eyes cast down)

RAMA: Will you wait for me, my love?

SITA: Will you look at me, my lord.

RAMA: *(Managing finally to bring his eyes to meet hers)* Will you wait until I return?

(Her eyes blaze with quiet anger. He is stunned as he has never seen defiance in her before)

SITA: Perhaps the dharma I learned in my father's house is different here in Ayhoda. I was taught that a wife's path is to share her husband's fate.If you must walk the Danaka Vana for 14 years – it will be with your wife at your side.

RAMA: Sita, don't be naive. You will die out there. It is no place for even the most savage of men.

SITA: *(Simply)* I am your wife in this life, and all the lives that follow. My place is by your side.

(VALMIKI 2 cleans the SITA-BODY. She begins to sing an old song of love)

RAMA: *(RAMA takes in the full measure of his wife and nods)* Janaki – we will walk together into the great darkness. May God watch over us and someday bring us home.

(They turn to KAUSALYA. She marks a tilaka on their brows and ties a raksha of protection around their wrists)

KAUSALYA: Go while I am still strong.

(RAMA and SITA turn to go. Once alone – KAUSALYA prostrates herself full length on the floor and weeps)

VALMIKI 2: *(To Audience)* Before day breaks, the three walk away from Ayhoda in silence: Lakshmana holds the lantern up ahead; Sita is at Rama's back; the horses that carry their few possessions will take them to the forest edge. And then they are on their own.

DASARATHA: *(Running after them, crying out with desperation)* Rama, Rama…

(He falls to his knees and begins to weep blood from his eyes. KAUSALYA pulls him into her arms)

(The twin boys cry out in their haunting song)

VALMIKI 2: How beautiful are the gardens of Ayhoda. How gentle the music we did not know we heard, until it is gone. Our breath in the dark, damp cavern of the mouth quickens, as blood moves through a heart now exiled from all it has known.

V.

(They have been riding for hours)

SITA: You spoke me through each town and village we passed.

RAMA: Now the lands Ikshvaku was given by his father in the krita yuga.

SITA: And with each step, Ayhoda behind us, fell backwards into our future dreams of longing for the past.

(RAMA turns his face to the North from where they have come)

RAMA: When will I see you again, beloved land of my ancestors? Seven years twice over I will be gone. An eternity for those we leave. But for the Devas, less than a single day.
God willing – some day I will come home.

(He lies face down and kisses the earth. LAKSHMANA and SITA do the same)

SITA: We released the horses to ride, empty saddled, across these great lands.

RAMA: Ride friends – back to Ayhoda. With you, take our souls.

SITA: We looked out at the magnificent waters of the Ganga. We knew, as darkness fell – that when we crossed the dark waters of that goddess in the morning – it would be many years, if ever, that we would return home.

RAMA: *(To SITA)* Soul of souls: Talk to us of the Ganga. I need her legend on my broken heart.

SITA: *(SITA speaks in a low voice, to the soporific swell and flow of the waters)* In times we can no longer recall – except in flickering shadows before we sleep – Himavan, the Emperor of mountains had two daughters. Uma was one. And Ganga the other. They say Ganga fell to us from the stars. She who flows at our feet is not only a river. But a Goddess who flows through our world.

(KUSA and LAVA's singing begins to build as SITA's tale fades. The VALMIKIS rub the dead SITA-BODY with a fine oil)

VALMIKI 1: How perfect are the city walls that once held us – before the fall. How soon we forget that the sand too has a voice; the trees command life on the sidewalks of every city; and that truly we all answer to the same name.

(A growing golden light)

When dawn broke – the brothers prepared for the great crossing over.

(RAMA and LAKSHMANA rise and apply the sticky milk of the pipal tree into their long hair. They coil their tangled locks onto their heads and change their clothes to the humblest of men. The transformation is stunning. They step into the boat)

SITA: *(As they move out onto Ganga's waters, SITA quietly prays)* Devi, Queen of that great body we call the ocean: Grant that in fourteen years, we will cross your waters again to come home.

VALMIKI 2: But as they move out into the deep, something stirs beneath. Somewhere, a shadowed figure opens its eyes and shakes off sleep. Again and again, through the ages, the darkness must be born.

(The VALMIKIS stretch the SITA-BODY out along the floor and cast water over the silent corpse. VALMIKI 2 steps away from the body and peels off her cloth to reveal a stunningly beautiful woman approaching middle age. This is MANDODARI. The STREET BOYS cry out their wild, beautiful song)

2: Fall

I.

(RAVANA rises from his bed and moves to a window. The ocean below swells and rages. Battle-scarred, lithe and terrifying – he is an extraordinary presence. Beautiful but inscrutable, his wife MANDODARI rises too and stands nearby, watching his back)

MANDODARI: Is there something my husband needs?

RAVANA: I dreamt of my Death… And she was beautiful.
(He turns, staring darkly at her)
A woman's damp sex over my eyes, an eagle's dense feather plunging to earth, sleeper on the timeless ocean, singing my name. And I wanted more…

MANDODARI: Come back to bed.

RAVANA: Yes. But not yours. Death dreams always make me hunger. And you alone will not suffice.

MANDODARI: *(Turning away)* As you please.
(Gripping her long dark hair, he pulls her towards him and forces her slowly to her knees. She stares up at him, a mixture of loathing and desire)

RAVANA: *(Smiling)* And I do please you, yes?

MANDODARI: *(A whisper)* Yes.

RAVANA: Why then, Queen of the Rakshasas… Why always the black light from your eyes?
(MANDODARI pulls away in disgust)

MANDODARI: You smell of your harem. Every one of your whores comes with you to my bed. They are on my sheets even after you are gone.

RAVANA: *(Pulling her up towards him from her knees, he violently tears away her robes. Suddenly his ten heads blossom on his shoulders. It is an awesome sight)* But I bring you great pleasure, yes?

MANDODARI: *(Despite herself)* Yes.

RAVANA: *(In her ear)* I still feel you as you closed on me for the first time as a child. How you drew my tide again and again. *(She cries out, overcome)* I know the anatomy of your surrender. It will always be mine.

(Pushing her brutally from him to the floor, where she covers her face with shame)

What I don't know…is when I will come for you again. Perhaps the next moon. Or the one after that. I cannot be precise.

MANDODARI: Don't go… *(MANDODARI holds onto him as he walks away)* Please. Come every day. Bring your whores.

(He pulls her face to within inches from his own)

RAVANA: Still Beautiful, Queen MANDODARI: My First. Older… but beautiful yet!

(He shakes her from him and leaves. She falls to the floor, weeping and feverish for him, furious with herself but helpless against the continued tide of her pain and lust after all these years. She composes herself to the empty room, rises and goes to the window, but buckles over and weeps again)

VALMIKI 1: One should never discount the beauty of Darkness. Even the Deva women fall to their knees in its embrace. For there is nothing as confounding as the pull of the great shadow. Out of it we are borne both away and towards ourselves.

II.

(RAMA, SITA and LAKSHMANA enter the forest. The VALMIKIS clean the feet of the SITA-BODY as they sing softly of paths that must be walked)

RAMA: Be calm. Danaka Vana will feed on whatever we feel.

(The performer who plays DASARATHA, with blood still covering his eyes, holds aloft a magnificent eagle who flies above them. LAKSHMANA raises his bow and aims at the bird, but RAMA touches his arm)

This is his home brother. *We* are the intruders here.

(They move forward into the dense foliage. The eagle never leaves them, flying above. Suddenly they stop dead in their tracks. In the clearing ahead – the bodies of women and children hang from the trees. SITA gasps and turns away)

LAKSHMANA: *(Bow raised, ready to attack)* In God's name who did this?

JATAYU: *(The eagle suddenly settles on a branch nearby)* We do not say his name.

SITA: Ravana of Lanka.

RAMA: We are Kshatriyas from the House of Ikshvaku. We would have come sooner…

(He cannot go on, overwhelmed by what they have seen)

JATAYU: We know who you are – Princes of Ayhoda. And Sita: Daughter to the Great Mother. We have been waiting for you through countless cycles. Everything painful that has led you this way, was an instrument in the unfolding plan. May it be ever blessed.

RAMA: You know who I am?

JATAYU: We do, Rama of Ayhoda.
Do you?

(RAMA stares at him, searching his ancient face. JATAYU stares back for the longest time)

LAKSHMANA: *(Still overwhelmed by the sight of the dead children and mothers)* This Ravana will know our names.

SITA: He is an expression of what lives in us all.

LAKSHMANA: *(Disgusted)* No one can say I have the murder of children in my soul, Janaki.

SITA: We don't know who we truly are, brother… until we survive that long night of the soul.

JATAYU: Child of the Dharma…

RAMA: Who are you, ancient one?

JATAYU: I am Jatayu. Your father sent me from where he cannot come.

(RAMA lays down his weapon, trembling with emotion. He gestures in deference to the great bird)

RAMA: Mighty one.

JATAYU: Danaka Vana is a complex nest of shadows. I offer what protection I can.

(JATAYU glances at LAKSHMANA, who has not yet returned his arrow to its quiver)

With my life – if you only ask.

(RAMA nods to LAKSHMANA, who – on RAMA's command – returns his arrow, and presses his hands together in deference to the bird)

RAMA: And we, the sons of the Ishvaku Line, give our word : We will not rest until we have ripped the dark by its roots, from these sacred soils.

JATAYU: Even if it is in yourselves that you find it thrives?

RAMA: *(Unnerved but steadfast)* Even so. We give our unbreakable word.

JATAYU: Follow closely. I will bring you to a clearing for the night.

SITA: *(With a last glance over their shoulders at the murdered women and children)* We follow you, Ancient one – with new fear yet hope in our hearts.

III.

(We find MANDODARI where we left her – bent over, weeping. She slowly stands erect and, with great dignity, rearranges herself. She looks at us)

MANDODARI: I cannot recall a time before I was his. A virgin child-bride when I first stood before him. His battle-scarred body was a map I could not follow. His dark, brutal hands calling me closer, closer still. In his harem-the most beautiful from all realms, joined in opening me – their long fingers reaching inside to steal my essence. An expert in tantra vidya – he searched relentlessly for every portal into what was not yet formed. I emerged from his harem though only days later – decades old. Insatiable to this day, he comes to me each dawn after dozens of women – wanting more, more, more.

In the hours between his visits – I am a child of water stranded on the mainland. What else have I been grown for? What am I if not his? I would rather he comes, bathed in the low tide pungent scent of other women than not come at all. We don't know the smell of the shadows – but that they compel us to sell ourselves again and again, just for one moment more.

(MANDODARI's long dark hair spreads like a web in RAVANA's fingers, as he draws her back helplessly into his embrace)

(She whispers) Forgive me.

RAVANA: Always. The tide of this body you inhabit, brought Indrajit to manifestation's shores. More than any – that boy has my proud, savage soul.

MANDODARI: But it is a girl child you still ache for. We have all failed you in this. Time and again we push out new life. But never yet the redemption of a baby girl: The tender antithesis to all your brutality in this world.

RAVANA: My queen knows me best. Sons – I have hundreds of… borne from these loins. *(He laughs with self-irony)* Perhaps in preparation for the ongoing wars of my own soul.

(MANDODARI watches him carefully, inscrutably as he walks away)

IV.

(RAMA's eyes search the dark – as the reality of the dangers around them becomes increasingly real. His despair is growing)

RAMA: How did I let you leave with me?
This is my Dharma to endure alone.

(He covers his face with his hands. They both turn to him and touch him tenderly)

SITA: Husband to me in this life, in all the lives that came before and those yet to come –

LAKSHMANA: I will find some fuel for the ring of fire we will need to keep the wild beasts away through the night.

(LAKSHMANA gathers wood and materials, and lights a ring of fire around the three of them. But SITA stands at the periphery of the fire. RAMA goes to her)

RAMA: What is it, my love?

SITA: Dharma is a tender thing, my Lord.

RAMA: *(Gently)* Go on.

SITA: I know you will protect me always. But promise me, Rama… Promise me you will never strike until struck. Dharma, my love, is peace – most of all.

RAMA: Janaki, those who dwell in the ashrams of this forest sitting tapasya, are the gatekeepers of the world. To protect them is the very reason fate has called me here.

SITA: My soul – I too am here for a reason: To watch over *your* dharma. I have known this since I first saw you at the river, washing blood from your hands as a boy. Your spirit is my charge. And always I will say to you: Life is sacred – even in the darkest of men.

RAMA: *(Taking her face in both his hands and looking her in the eyes)* Janaki, every sorrow we have lived, is a dark thread leading to my true purpose here.

SITA: You know I do not frighten easily, Rama. But something wild has been awakened. It lurks around the corners of these, our bright days. And I feel more fear than I ever have in my life.

(LAKSHMANA appears again from the dark)

LAKSHMANA: Forgive me for intruding. Something moves swiftly this way. I felt its pulse in the earth as I lay down. It will be here soon.

RAMA: Take Janaki to the cave we saw earlier and wait there with her, brother. I will do this alone.

SITA: Rama…

RAMA: This is what the Dharma brought me here for, soul. This is only the beginning.

(To LAKSHMANA) Go.

(After a beat, SITA nods and allows LAKSHMANA to lead her away, leaving RAMA alone in the circle of fire. We feel the pulse as the threat moves across the forest towards him. With a bow in his quiver, he stands ready)

V.

(RAVANA is eating with relish. His brother, VIBHEESHANA waits silently for his response to the news he has brought. MANDODARI stands nearby watching the exchange)

RAVANA: How many?

VIBHEESHANA: Every one of our fourteen thousand is fallen, my Lord.

RAVANA: Gifted though they must be to have razed Khara's invincible army – they do not know Ravana of Lanka. They will pay a brutal price.

VIBHEESH: Not "they" my Lord – but "he."

(All ten heads rise and swivel to look at VIBHEESHANA. The effect is astounding. Though he is used to his brother, VIBHEESHANA shrinks in terror)

One man, with bow and arrow alone, killed them all.

(The ten faces begin to hiss. It is a terrifying sound. Then each head begins to talk at once)

RAMA: A mortal?

VIBHEESH: Rama of Ayhoda. His lineage is the noble race of Surya; From the Royal House of Ikshvaku.

(RAMA, inside the ring of fire, defends himself against the onslaught)

We – the handful who survived – no longer sleep. The calm beauty of his face haunts me still.

(RAMA stops fighting and looks around at the ground strewn with corpses. Shimmering petals rain down on him as he stands perfectly still)

(RAVANA moves to the window and stares out at the sea below)

RAVANA: I do not usually extend this honour – but I will go to Janasthana to kill this "Blue Prince" myself.

VIBHEESH: Lord of all the Worlds, hear me: He shone like a God when he faced our army. Through it all – he barely took a breath.

RAVANA: Are you saying this mortal is beyond me, brother?

VIBHEESH: I am saying: This is a mortal... But no ordinary man.

(Suddenly and quietly, MANDODARI speaks)

MANDODARI: Nothing is beyond you, Lord of all the worlds.

(They both turn, in astonishment, to listen to her. She has never spoken to RAVANA of matters beyond her limited role)

RAVANA: *(Intrigued)* Speak. You have my ear.

MANDOR: Rama has a wife – Sita. She who followed her husband into the forest when a lesser woman would have forsaken a man. Sita, whom Rama of Ayhoda loves more than his own life. They are one another's prana, Lord.

RAVANA: Go on...

MANDOR: The apsaras of Devaloka are no match for her beauty. Her face a work of art – her body a vision. We must have her Ravana. While that woman is in the world, there should be no peace until the most powerful being in this realm makes her his own.

VIBHEESH: *(With quiet outrage)* Mandodari, there is no greater sin than to steal a man's wife.

MANDOR: *(Ignoring VIBHEESHANA, she continues)* If you were to abduct the beautiful Sita – not only would the most exquisite woman in the three worlds complete our Harem... But Rama of Ayhoda would be conquered. His heart...

RAVANA: *(His dark eyes, glittering, fixed on MANDODARI)* Cleft in two.

MANDOR: Rama has made the fatal error you never would. He truly loves a woman. No skill on the battlefield, no cunning or brute strength, can protect one from grief. Slow, unfolding grief that gently but inevitably kills.

(All ten of RAVANA's heads turn to look at her. They begin to smile. He pulls MANDODARI to him. VIBHEESHANA backs away and out, leaving them alone. RAVANA tears her clothes from her and repeats SITA's name, like a mantra, over and over again)

VI.

(DASARATHA stands in a mule cart. He has a garland of wild flowers around his neck. He is slowly pulling the long white hair out his head. He tears his clothes away until he stands naked, old and frail in the wind)

(SITA lies beside RAMA, turning in her sleep. We see that DASARATHA is the vision she dreams)

(DASARATHA cups dark soil to his mouth and eats)

(SITA starts awake. She cries out)

RAMA: What is it, Sita?

SITA: *(Looking at RAMA and LAKSHMANA)* Dasaratha.

LAKSHMANA: Sita, you were dreaming.

SITA: Sons of the Ikshvaku Line: Your Father is dead.

(RAMA walks away into the dark, knowing it is true. He falls to his knees. LAKSHMANA goes to RAMA)

LAKSHMANA: Brother…

RAMA: There is no Ayhoda for me now.

LAKSHMANA: Your people wait for you Rama.

RAMA: What other man has lived that once held my small hand in his.

(He waits until RAMA's weeping subsides. He touches him gently)

LAKSHMANA: Let us offer tarpana.

(RAMA looks at his brother. Slowly he nods, gathering himself. The VALMIKIS sway and hum an old song of despair. RAMA wades into

the river until he is waist deep. LAKSHMANA follows but stays at a distance in the water. SITA watches from the shore. RAMA faces south and raises his arms to the skies)

RAMA: Father, you have been gathered back to the Father's in Pitriloka.

LAKSHMANA: Dasaratha of Ikshvaku: we eat this fruit in your name. Your sons thank you for the gift of life and swear to honour you to our last breath.

(The brothers eat the fruit. RAMA gives some to SITA. They rise and begin to walk. LAKSHMANA walks ahead)

RAMA: Janaki, I am lost…

SITA: *(She takes his face in her hands)*
But not alone. I walk beside you, Lord Rama.
In this life and those to come…
I am yours.

(She kisses his eyes, like she did when she met him as a boy)

(The twin boys sing out as we see dawn break. RAMA and LAKSHMANA worship the new sun with Suryanamaskaru)

SITA: Danaka Vana came to trust us, as we did it. Lakshmana built us a humble home in the deepest part of the wild. And one could say – without restraint – that we were happy. Were we not beloved? Were those not our sweetest years? Outside of our sanctuary, the genocide continued like a dark beast rolling downhill. You tried to protect me from what lay beyond the light. But I have always understood sorrow, my beloved. It was sorrow that led me under my father's city wall to find you as a girl. It is sorrow, after all, that drew me to the golden creature. Her sorrowful eyes looked into my soul.

I have been held much responsible for what happened next. And though they will say it is the woman's heart easily drawn to temptation… she sang to me of sorrow. And I answered her call. I would rather mistake evil for sorrow a million times over – than walk away in fear from something that cries out for help.

(RAVANA stands between shadows and shafts of light. LAVA and KUSA sing in low tones, as RAVANA opens his dark coat, releasing an exquisite, shimmering deer. SITA is stunned by its other-worldly beauty. It comes toward and nuzzles her. She is transfixed)

SITA: Who are you, fine one? From what part of me?

(RAMA and LAKSHMANA come up behind her)

RAMA: Whose work is this?

SITA: *(She moves again towards the creature and notices it is weeping silent tears)* Why do you weep, child? What sorrows are yours?

LAKSHMANA: *(Backing away)* No animal of this realm weeps. Brother, now is the time to be awake.

SITA: I am gifted to hear the voices of all creatures – but yours is silent to me. Why?

RAMA: *(Looking at SITA with the same love she looks with upon the deer)*

(To LAKSHMANA) Never have I known a person to encompass such compassion for all life.

LAKSHMANA: Brother wake up. You are both enchanted:

(The animal suddenly darts away from SITA into the thick of the forest)

SITA: Rama – she is new born and not yet steady on her feet. The wild beasts will have her before night. Save her. I beg you, beloved.

LAKSHMANA: Brother, hear me! This is no earthly creature. Her beauty smells dark.

RAMA: If you are right – I will know it when I have her and I will kill her without a moment's pause. If she is who Sita believes her to be – a foundling needing protection like she once was – then Sita will have the only thing she has ever asked of me. Do not leave her for even a moment. I will be back soon with the golden creature – either dead in my arms or walking by my side.

SITA: Find her, Rama. Or we are lost.

(RAMA nods, and moves off swiftly into the thick of the forest. He turns back once, waves to SITA – and is gone)

SITA: *(Becoming lucid, emerging from the trance)* Brother, that creature conjured my own ancient grief. I recalled myself at both birth and death, in a furrow of earth, waiting to be found.

(LAKSHMANA is silent. His grave concern hangs in the air)

SITA: Have I sent Rama to great danger?

LAKSHMANA: I believe you have, Sita... yes.

(RAMA pursues the golden deer. It is a complex and beautiful pursuit, as the shimmering creature moves between shafts of light in the the dark of the forest. RAMA raises his bow several times – but is moved to pity and lowers his weapon. Suddenly the creature stops and RAMA sees, in his mind's eye, SITA as she waved goodbye to him. In SITA's voice, the deer suddenly speaks a single, chilling line)

SITA as DEER: The gate is open – and she is lost.

(RAMA's face is suddenly stricken with panic for, in an instant, he understands all)

RAMA: NO! *(He shoots the deer through the heart, and cries out in warning)* SITA! LAKSHMANA!!!

(He begins running back to their sanctuary, but dark has fallen and in his pursuit of the deer he had wandered further than he thought. He stumbles, groping blindly as the roots and branches of the trees reach out to restrain him. He fights ferociously, calling out)

SITA! LAKSHMANA!

(They both turn in the direction of RAMA's cry)

SITA: That was my Rama. Go to him, Lakshmana! Fly!

LAKSHMANA: I gave Rama my word I would not leave your side.

SITA: Go to him or he will die.

(A shadow crosses over her face. She steps back in horror)

You want him dead to make me yours!

LAKSHMANA: Janaki, calm yourself...

SITA: *(Turning her burning eyes onto him)* I have known it always. I have seen you watching me… In the mornings at the river when I wash. You have waited patiently for this day! You are a blot on the Ikshvaku name!

(LAKSHMANA looks at her – devastated like a child)

Somewhere in your soul's darkest reach – you want your brother dead.

(LAKSHMANA presses his hands over his eyes in agony at this decision. Then he moves suddenly around SITA, and draws a circle of light)

LAKSHMANA: Stay within this circle. It will hold you until I return. If you break beyond it, I cannot bring you back again into light.

(Looking her in the eyes)

May God forgive you Janaki.
May God forgive us both.

(LAKSHMANA turns and disappears into the forest in the direction of RAMA's voice)

(SITA chants the Vedas softly to herself – trying to contain her panic. She hears a deep sigh)

SITA: Who is there in the dark?

(RAVANA steps out of the shadows. SITA steps back in fear. RAVANA is searching her face – utterly transfixed)

RAVANA: I am lost.

SITA: *(Looking deeply into his eyes)* Yes.

(They stand like that for a long time. RAMA, in his battle with the forest, calls out – but SITA can no longer hear him)

RAMA: *(Calling out desperately)* Sita! SITA!

RAVANA: May I come nearer.

SITA: I am protected by the Rekha's circle of light.

(RAVANA falls to his knees. He is weeping. He covers his face in shame)

Why do you weep?

RAVANA: In your eyes, I see myself as I am.

SITA: And who are you?

RAVANA: Ravana of Lanka.

(*SITA steps back in naked terror, but the compassion does not leave her eyes*)

SITA: You have much to weep for, Ravana of Lanka. I have seen your work.

RAVANA: I am backwards standing before you. I am at the bottom of the ocean as you whisper to me, floating through currents of time. I want to weep and I know not why, but that you look at me as the man I was before Ravana of Lanka became my name. I want to lie at your feet and for you to find me another name.

SITA: Names are but shifting shadows.

RAVANA: Everything but my name is long dead.
(*Proudly*) I am the Rakshasa that conquered the world.

SITA: And this brings you joy?

RAVANA: It brings me power.
You bring me home. Every man wants to be forgiven by she who sees him anew.

SITA: The essence remains, no matter how far we have wandered.

RAVANA: You are wrong, daughter. Some of us are lost, forever.

SITA: And in saying so – found again.

RAVANA: Let me take the dust from your feet.

SITA: It's not possible. The circle protects me.

RAVANA: If my essence of good remains, why then do you need protection?
(*She hesitates*)

Beautiful words of faith… but hollow, my dear.
(*She looks up sharply*)

Forgive me. I would not trust me either.

(He turns to go)

SITA: I …

RAVANA: For a short time while you looked at me – I remembered who I once was.

SITA: Come let me bless you, Ravana of Lanka. Let me offer faith where there has been none. You have destroyed countless lives in this realm but if I forgive you, then surely we all rise.

RAVANNA: You are trembling.

SITA: I am deeply afraid. But you are too.

(SITA steps out of the occult circle and it starts to fade)

VALMIKI 2: *(Sighs)* And so like a stone rolling downhill, destiny takes its course: The abduction into darkness of the self.

(LAKSHMANA and RAMA running wildly, collide. They grab each other and begin to wrestle ferociously. Realizing their error, they stop and look at each other)

RAMA: *(Grabbing LAKSHMANA)* Where is she? Brother, where is Janaki?

LAKSHMANA: She heard you cry out! She would not let me stay with her, but insisted I come to protect your life.

RAMA: I TOLD YOU NEVER TO LEAVE HER SIDE! O god! O dear god! Janaki…

(He runs back towards the sanctuary, calling her name. LAKSHMANA follows. They come to the fading, empty circle of light)

RAMA: What have you done? *(Shaking his brother who is weeping like a child)*

LAKSHMANA: Forgive me, brother. Forgive me…

(RAMA grabs LAKSHMANA in a fierce embrace as he weeps)

RAMA: O god brother… What have we done?

(The STREET URCHINS – KUSA and LAVA – cry out, as lights fade)

3. Monkey Mind

I.

(Lights grow on HANUMAN: A magnificent half monkey-half man. A soft piece of fabric from Sita's clothing floats down from above. He reaches out with one hand and effortlessly catches it. He looks up to where it came from)

HANUMAN: She is beauty that can only be spoken of in the voices of the rain. Golden of skin, hair like seaweed from the deepest ocean-leagues below where no light is seen. Yet it is the compassion in her lotus eyes that sets her apart. Borne of the great mother herself, there can be no doubt.

(Lights grow further and we realize he is talking to SUGRIVA. A monkey-man like HANUMAN)

SUGRIVA: Forget you ever saw her taken. She is a whisper in the halls of Lanka now.

HANUMAN: She is Sita. Wife to Rama of Ayhoda.

(SUGRIVA turns in astonishment to look at HANUMAN – then turns away, shaking his head)

SUGRIVA: Ravana of Lanka has any woman he wants. Long ago he was cursed never to force himself on a woman again. And so he has learnt to garden subverted desire and rob the essence of even the strongest feminine soul. Forget Rama, Hanuman. His wife belongs to Ravana now.

HANUMAN: *(Daring himself to be frank)* My Lord – you know what it is to lose everything! To be exiled from your mother land and have your woman taken into the night.

(SUGRIVA is silent. The mention of his own exile and lost wife have pierced him to the core. He waits for the pain to flow away. HANUMAN stands quietly – unsure how SUGRIVA will take his naming the unmentionable. Finally SUGRIVA speaks)

SUGRIVA: Find Rama of Ayhoda and bring him to me.

(HANUMAN turns and is lifted into the arms of his father – the wind)

II.

(RAMA and LAKSHMANA are moving through the forest, searching for SITA. RAMA is frantic with despair. We have never seen him like this)

RAMA: *(To the trees. to the river)* Have you seen her – ancient ones? Did you see where Sita went?

LAKSHMANA: Brother, no one saw her go.

RAMA: *(To the mountain, in rage)* Tell me what you saw! You have been here since before time - but I swear, I will end you! I am Rama of Ayhoda... SPEAK!

(Stumbling to his knees, he holds his head in his hands. He begins to weep)

LAKSHMANA: Rama, be calm. Nothing will come of losing yourself.

RAMA: *(To LAKSHMANA, with chilling resolve)* From today I am another man! With my hands I will tear the earth down to its core. I will turn the sun to ash and silence the stars. Darkness will reign – until Sita is again by my side.

(RAMA draws an awesome shaft from his quiver, and begins fitting it to his bowstring. LAKSHMANA falls at his feet)

LAKSHMANA: I beg you, Rama. This is not the way of the Dharma!

(A gust of wind blows a mass of feathers that fly about his feet. RAMA drops his bow and stumbles along a trail of blood. They find JATAYU dying nearby)

RAMA: Noblest friend…

JATAYU: Lord Rama. Sita has been taken South.

RAMA: By whom, ancient warrior?

JATAYU: I swore to protect her. But I am old and he stormed the skies.

RAMA: Who took my Sita?

JATAYU: Hold me Rama. I am going into the great darkness now.

(RAMA takes the magnificent bird in his arms as he dies)

LAKSHMANA: *(Looking at the silent and still RAMA with new awareness)* Brother, for a moment – I was more afraid of you than anyone I have ever known. You are more than I ever guessed. More than I can know.

(RAMA says nothing. He stares fiercely into the gathering storm)

III.

(SITA lies unconscious in a dank cell. RAVANA crawls towards her – serpentine – along the floor. Elevating himself on his arms above her. She shifts and he backs away suddenly into a corner. SITA wakes, looks around with growing fear and then finds RAVANA staring at her from the dark corner)

RAVANA: My love…

SITA: *(With terrified, dawning comprehension that she has been abducted)* No…no…where is Rama? What is this place?

RAVANA: You will love me, Sita…

SITA: Mother, mother, mama, ma…I cannot keep back this tide. I do not have the strength…

RAVANA: Let me be strong for us. I am fiercer than the mind can hold.

(But SITA is not talking to him. She seems to be communing – in her terror – with another presence)

SITA: This is the Lingam without Yoni. This is the power without its base; The force of the pull without the moon's balance. Great Mother, this is the Shiva-Linga that can no longer see itself.

RAVANA: I will lie and die in you. Push my way through.

SITA: Rama, find me! Or we are all lost.

(RAVANA moves towards her. SITA picks up a blade of grass and points it at him. RAVANA clutches at his groin and backs away. He begins to weep, with pain and desire, like a child)

SITA: Mother, he cannot see the Yoni at the base. The sacred balance forever lost…

We will stumble in his questions for long ages. Darkness will spread until Shiva-Linga stands where Yoni can never resume her place.

(RAVANA holds himself, weeping. Finally he stands over her)

RAVANA: I am the golden deer you sent Rama into the darkness to pursue. You brought this upon yourself. Now or later you will know the depth of your own desire. And when you do – you will never want to find your way home again.

(He turns and walks away from SITA who stares at the wall trying to contain her pure, naked terror)

IV.

(RAMA and LAKSHMANA have been stumbling through the forest for days, searching for SITA. HANUMAN observes them for some time from a hiding place. RAMA kneels in the earth and begins to chant the Vedas through gritted teeth, but is soon overwhelmed)

(The VALMIKIS watch impassively from the periphery)

VALMIKI 2: Into the belly of the great Danaka Vana we must all drift alone. Our only means of navigation: the chattering monkeys of the mind! But amongst them lives devotion – waiting to be harnessed and quietly heard.

HANUMAN: *(Stepping out to reveal himself)* Brothers, why have you come to this desolate place?

LAKSHMANA: *(On the defense, with bow raised)* Who is asking?

(HANUMAN reaches out and offers RAMA the fabric from SITA's dress. RAMA stumbles back. LAKSHMANA slowly takes it from HANUMAN. Then instantly raising his bow again)

This is Sita's. How do you come to have it?

HANUMAN: Some days ago – the sky was filled with her cries. I looked up to see a Rakshasa with a woman in his arms, struggling for her life. What she dropped, floated like a broken wing, into my open palm.

(RAMA holds the fabric, lost in the touch and scent of SITA)

LAKSHMANA: Who are you? For whom do you speak?

HANUMAN: I am Hanuman – son of the Wind God Varayu. Sugriva sent me to find you.

LAKSHMANA: Sugriva, once King of the Vanaras?

HANUMAN: You have heard his story?

LAKSHMANA: I have heard that he is just and true.

HANUMAN: Driven from his Kingdom by his brother Vali, his wife and home stolen from him –

Sugriva lives as an outcast now – fearing everyday his brother will come for his life.

(RAMA is quiet for some time. He finally lifts his head and speaks)

RAMA: If your King Sugriva and his Vanaras will help me find Sita – I will do the bloodletting he cannot.

LAKSHMANA: *(Taking RAMA aside)* Rama, this trouble between brothers is none of our concern…Remember your promise to Sita, my Lord!

RAMA: Just as you knew you must follow me into the Wild…I know my Dharma is to walk where Hanuman leads me today.

(LAKSHMANA is silenced by this thought)

(To HANUMAN) Take me to Sugriva. He is my brother in grief.

VALMIKI 1: Monkey heart. Monkey mind. The carousel of endless possibilities turning in the vortex of longing. And then one sharp morning – devotion walks into our field, drops to the soil and begins planting new seeds.

(As the VALMIKIS turn the SITA-BODY over, they sing of HANUMAN's devotion, and sponge the lifeless SITA-BODY)

V.

(RAMA and SUGRIVA fiercely embrace. LAKSHMANA and HANUMAN stand silently, watching over the lives they have each devoted themselves to. SITA, in her far off confinement, finds refuge in her vedas. Beneath her chanting, we hear SUGRIVA by the fire, telling RAMA his story)

SUGRIVA: For many years there was great love between me and Vali – much like between you *(referring to Lakshmana)* and your blood here. Vali was older brother to me – but equally Father, Soul's Friend and Guru. I have loved him since before we were both conceived. When Vali grew to be King – I wanted only to serve him with my life. One night, an Asura challenged my brother over a woman. We of monkey mind, are ruled by the passions of our blood. To kill over a woman is, for us, not an uncommon thing. When the Asura saw me and Vali coming for him in the full moon's light – he fled into the forest and vanished into a cave. Vali told me to guard the entrance as he went in. I waited at the cave mouth for hours, which turned to days, then weeks and months! I ate only what the nearby trees offered. I hardly slept. But one night – after ninety-two moons, I heard Vali scream. A stream of blood – dark like a vanara's – flowed from the cave at my feet. I rolled a boulder over the entrance and ran for my life. Back in Kishkinda, I offered tarpana to my dead brother's spirit and, still grieving, was crowned by Vali's ministers who thought he would never return.

One morning months later, I woke to find Vali standing over my bed. He was exhausted but alive. I wept for joy. But he stripped the blankets from me and looked only at the the golden rings on my toes, and the crown beside my bed. "Murderer" he whispered with burning eyes, and chased me through the three worlds. This mountain is the one place Vali is cursed not to set foot. And so I hide here. He lives as King now. He sleeps between my wife's legs, with my homeland and future in his hands. If I leave the sanctity of this mountain, he will hunt me down and make me pay for a kingdom I never stole... but one which was given to me by those who thought he would never return.

(SUGRIVA is weeping. RAMA holds him in an embrace again)

RAMA: Take me to your brother, Vali. It's time to go home.

(A memory of SITA appears at RAMA's right shoulder)

SITA: Promise me, my love! Promise me.
Dharma is peace – most of all.

RAMA: *(Looking over his shoulder)* Sita?

(But he is alone)

(KUSA and LAVA sing in their dissonant tones, as SITA – in her cell – reaches towards the moonlight streaming in from a small window)

VI.

(SUGRIVA stands opposite VALI. They face each other, locked in a mutual stare. A deep rumbling growl emanates from them both. The effect is awesome and ominous)

VALI: Have you grown so tired of exile that you prefer to die?

SUGRIVA: When will you know it was your own ministers who crowned me.

VALI: If you come seeking forgiveness – leave now with your life.

SUGRIVA: I am ready to die or kill you… rather than live this exile another day.

(VALI roars with laughter)

VALI: You are powerful, Sugriva – but you do not have my stamina. You will grow tired and stumble under one of my blows. But unlike when we were children – I will not lift you from the earth, dust you off and help you home.

SUGRIVA: I will always love you, brother.

(VALI is stone-faced and silent. SUGRIVA nods)

The will of the gods be done.

(The two collide with terrifying force. The fight is on. Their strokes are powerful, their blows deadly. They are equally matched in force but soon, SUGRIVA begins to tire. VALI strikes him three times. SUGRIVA's knees buckle. RAMA steps out from where he was hidden, and places a

quiver in his bow. He looks behind him. Is it SITA watching him from the shadows?)

RAMA: Sita?

SITA: My soul – I am here to watch over your dharma. I have known this since I first saw you at the river, washing blood from your hands.

RAMA: Sugriva has enough Vanaras to cover the earth's face searching for you. I will do what must be done.

(In one move, he shoots VALI through the heart. The powerful monkey-man falls to the earth with thunderous impact. SUGRIVA moves to his dying brother's side. He lies gasping, blood flowing from his mouth. RAMA kneels in prayer. The spectre of SITA walks slowly away. RAMA takes VALI in his arms)

VALI: Have I died?

RAMA: You are going, Great One. But not yet gone.

VALI: My life becomes a thin and fading thing. Is it you – Blue One of Grace – that holds me at the gateway?

RAMA: It is Rama who holds you, and Rama who killed you, my friend.

VALI: *(In disbelief)* You took it upon yourself to string your bow with my death... *(Overcome with emotion)* Is it true – Rama of Impeccable Dharma?

RAMA: It is you that has broken Dharma, monkey king.

(SUGRIVA weeps silently at VALI's side, but VALI stares only at RAMA – as though he is seeing a vision. RAMA begins to glow incandescently. It is VALI's dying image of him)

VALI: *(Smiling)* Ah! Look...

SUGRIVA: *(Seeing his brother's face luminous with vision)* What do you see, brother?

VALI: I see my way out of this broken body. Realms opening that were hidden from me before. You give me a path out of the bondage of this broken body – now that I know, dark prince, who you are.

RAMA: Who I am?

VALI: Yes! *(VALI is smiling, lost in his vision and slipping away)*

RAMA: WHO?

(But VALI only turns to SUGRIVA with a gentle smile)

VALI: We will meet again, brother. Look for me. I am there.

(VALI exhales for a last time and dies. SUGRIVA kneels and holds VALI. He weeps over the empty body of his brother. Thunder rumbles in the ever-darkening sky. RAMA is deeply shaken)

SUGRIVA: I will wait always at life's cave for you – until my own end.

HANUMAN: *(To RAMA and LAKSHMANA)* The Monsoons are come. I will show you our cave beneath the mountains where you will pass these months until the rains end.

RAMA: I will be waiting word from Sugriva that he has found where my Sita is held. I ache for the future… But this is the waiting season. May the gods give me strength.

SUGRIVA: *(Lifting VALI's body and carrying it into the driving rain)* Come with me brother. It's time to go home.

(SUGRIVA roars with grief, as the sky explodes with rain)

VII.

(RAVANA is slumped in his throne, with a hand over his eyes. His son INDRAJIT stands beside him. Enter VIBHEESHANA)

VIBHEESHANA: Brother, may I approach?

(RAVANA – without uncovering his eyes – nods. VIBHEESHANA moves in)

Rama has created a powerful alliance with the Vanaras under Sugriva…

INDRAJIT: You are mistaken. The Vanaras are ruled by Vali.

VIBHEE: No longer. Rama of Ayhoda has slain Vali and placed Sugriva back on the throne.

(RAVANA looks up astonished, but gathers himself immediately)

RAVANA: And in return for this "magnanimous" deed?

VIBHEE: Sugriva has sworn to avenge those who stole The Blue
Prince's woman.

RAVANA: And Rama of Ayhoda is where?

VIBHEE: He awaits news in an undisclosed cave until the
Monsoons end. It is said he who took his woman will know
the white flame of his wrath.

(RAVANA mocks a shudder and smiles at his son. INDRAJIT laughs –
searching his father's face)

VIBHEE: Tell me brother: Is she worth it?

(RAVANA looks up sharply)

– That you would allow the black song of doubt to enter
your closest consorts. That they whisper amongst themselves
"Ravana is drowning, like a woman, in sentiment and courts
his own death". Is she worth your death?

RAVANA: *(Dropping all sarcasm)* Brother, she recalls in me the dark
lullabies of our mother's despair. I drift towards the end of the
ravine with my eyes closed. I float. I fall into dark waters. I
must have what lives beneath there.

INDRAJIT: *(Deeply unnerved)* Why does my father – Lord of all the
Worlds – not simply TAKE what is his?

(RAVANA breathes deeply, closes his eyes and is quiet. VIBHEESHANA
stares at him, seeing the truth)

VIBHEE: *(Understanding, for the first time, just how lost his brother is)*
Because your father is cursed never to force himself on a
woman again.
Besides… lust alone is not what this is…

(RAVANA looks at his brother, startled at being exposed – and then
surrenders, closing his eyes again)

INDRAJIT: *(Urgently, beginning to lose control)* Father, she will never
love you. But there is no reason to lose everything simply
because she resists. Your longing is simply desire thwarted.
You yourself taught me this. Enter her daily – violently – until,

to you, she is any other whore. There is nothing like lust sated…to break the Sentimental Spell.

VIBHEE: *(Raising his voice to INDRAJIT)* THIS IS THE WIFE OF RAMA OF AYHODA! Not some CHILD of war your father has orphaned, with whom he can now do as he will!

INDRAJIT: *(Stunned by VIBHEESHANA's tone)* Mind yourself, old man. You forget who I am.

VIBHEE: *(Treading carefully, for INDRAJIT is indeed powerful)* I forget nothing, glorious warrior. But let there be no doubt…Yama waits in the shadows of this longing.

INDRAJIT: Sita will soon burn for his touch – like all the Whores that came before. But what would you know of such things, uncle? You are not like the men of our line. You have always carried the compassion of a woman. How convenient to be afforded such luxury: We must walk the battle fields, while you languish in moral dilemma at home!

VIBHEE: Hear me. Sita is the fire that will consume Lanka. Her husband comes in upon us from a timeless void borne of ages we will never master or know.

INDRAJIT: You speak with Indrajit – named so when he conquered the King of the Devas. If Rama of Ayhoda ever finds these shores – he will face me and he will know my true name.

VIBHEE: Rama of Lanka will tutor you in what I and even your father cannot.

INDRAJIT: He is a mortal. WE are Rakshasas. Do you forget what this means?

RAVANA: Meghanada –

INDRAJIT: It has been a long time since you have used my original name.

RAVANA: Meghanada – whose birth cry sounded like thunder. *(Lost in his thoughts, barely listening to his son and brother's conversation)*

INDRAJIT: How can I serve my Father... My King?

(*RAVANA beckons him to come close. He bends to catch RAVANA's soft words*)

RAVANA: I will have her eyes change just once for me, the way they do when she speaks his name. Do this for me. Destroy what stands in love's way.

INDRAJIT: (*Desperately, with rage*) Father...

(*But RAVANA has withdrawn again, hand over his eyes. VIBHEESHANA leads INDRAJIT away*)

VIBHEE: He is lost.
Ready all that can possibly hold back the tide that will soon move in.

VIII.

(*RAMA lies on his back in a cave listening to the storm raging outside. The SITA-BODY moves around him as a shadow, then lays full length on him. He starts awake. LAKSHMANA is sleeping at his side. Time passes. Water drips in the cave as the seconds, hours, weeks, months pass. All the while, the monsoons fall powerfully outside. RAMA strikes the wall and cries out at the pain. LAKSHMANA sits up and watches him*)

LAKSHMANA: Be patient brother...

RAMA: (*Beginning to lose control*) Where is she, brother? With whom does she spend her nights?

LAKSHMANA: Sugriva has surely sent his vanaras through the three worlds to find her. We will soon have news.

RAMA: I don't have the strength for doing nothing, brother.

LAKSHMANA: (*Coming to him with infinite compassion, he holds him by his shoulders*) We cannot know why – but there is an enemy whom destiny has set against you.
Sita is the river that draws us all towards a battlefield for reasons larger than your love – for we are instruments of the Dharma. No more or less.
Now let us think only of finding her – and bring her home.

RAMA: *(Gathering himself)* My brother, my soul's friend…
Finest amongst all men.

(RAMA embraces LAKSHMANA. They step back and look at each other as the world turns)

IX.

(SUGRIVA lies inebriated in the stupor of wine. HANUMAN prods him awake)

HANUMAN: You have your kingdom back, your wife, your life. You swore to Rama you would begin when the monsoons had passed! My Lord – what keeps you?

SUGRIVA: *(Drunk)* And have they passed, Son of the Wind? I am certain I still hear water's feet dancing pitter pat along the roof.

HANUMAN: The moon hangs low in a clear sky. It has been peaceful Sharada for more than a month. While you have been happy at wine and love, Rama counts not the seasons – but each moment of his life that passes without his beloved. Now is the time to call our Vanaras to comb the face of the earth for Rama's wife!

SUGRIVA: I need yet time to climb back into the world.

HANUMAN: I would not delay, my Lord. Lest Rama's love turn to rage.

(SUGRIVA looks frightened but does not move)

SUGRIVA: It has been many grievous years of waiting to come home. I am taking the time to heal, Hanuman.

HANUMAN: A warrior with death on his brow has arrived in our city. Lakshmana – brother to Rama of Ayhoda waits at the gate.

(SUGRIVA's smile fades. He grows very still)

SUGRIVA: Show him in.

(SUGRIVA rises from his bed. LAKSHMANA enters. He stands silently – pale with rage)

VALMIKI 2: "The body is not me and I not the body" the truth whispers. But gets lost all the same. "How beautiful is the song of wine and women?" she whispers, as we fall into the dark embrace.

LAKSHMANA: *(Quietly, with deadly rage)* The portal through which Vali left this world is yet open for you to follow. Honour your promise, before despair becomes my master and I kill you, Vanara.

(SUGRIVA begins to weep. He prostrates himself before LAKSHMANA, touching his feet)

SUGRIVA: Now you see the limits of the monkey-mind. Forgive me – I beg you. I cannot be what I am not.

LAKSHMANA: You gave Rama your word.
We of the Ishvaku line – hold nothing deeper than giving our word.

SUGRIVA: *(SUGRIVA, now fully lucid to the failed promises he made, turns to HANUMAN)* Summon my Vanaras from every jungle's corner. Those who do not come will die. *(To LAKSHMANA)* I will not fail your brother again. We will find his Sita – or may the Vanaras be cursed to search without pause – to the end of time.

X.

(RAVANA stands over SITA, looking down at her on the floor of the cell. She does not look at him but chants her Vedas repeatedly, rocking and looking into the cupped palms of her hands, held close to her face)

RAVANA: *(Inhaling deeply)* I smell you. I want you. More than any woman I have known in this realm.

(SITA will not look at him)

You don't know what it is to be in my embrace, Sita. Taste me. I will give you my all.

(She quietly continues chanting the vedas)

Many have longed to capture my dark heart… But you scorn it!

(Suddenly, he grabs her and drags her to her feet, through his halls and to a window where the ocean roars below)

All of this…I give it to you.

(Though she is shaking violently, she has a calm smile on her lips. He grasps her from behind and forces her face towards the magnificent view of Lanka)

I am the Emperor of ten million Rakshasas across the earth. All of them will be your subjects. You will have glory and power beyond your dreams. The thousand pieces of my harem shall be your handmaids. I will never touch one of them again if you ask this of me.

(He falls to his knees in front of her. She remains unmoved. He covers his ears)

It is a childhood song I hear, since I first saw you, before waking.
My mother entering and leaving a room as cold as your heart.
I want to lie in your arms and weep until sleeping.

SITA: *(She looks him in the eyes for the first time. She moves in closer)* What you do not know – Rakshasa – is that you are looking at your own death.

RAVANA: *(They hold each other's stare. Then quietly – with his own lethal power)* You have 100 days to consider my love. If you accept – you will be Queen of the three worlds. If you refuse –

(His ten heads appear. It is a grotesque and awesome sight. SITA is struck dumb)

I will bring pain your fragile body has never known. I will take you as mine – so violently that your insides will bleed from every portal your body owns.

SITA: It is known you are cursed never to force yourself on a woman again.

RAVANA: *(Smiling darkly)* But I love you, you see. How may I show you the lengths I am willing to go to? I will dance in the dark face of this curse. If its my last act of violence in this world, I will tear into you – body and soul.

SITA: You will be ash, Rakshasa, when you face the power of my vratas!

Do what you will. The soul is untouchable. And this body is but a passing thing.

(RAVANA grabs SITA and pulls her towards him but he is unhinged. He throws her to the ground. To his own astonishment, he finds his face wet with tears)

RAVANA: Don't look at me. *(He roars with rage)* LOOK AWAY! *(She looks down – for he is ferocious)* By love or by force – in a hundred days – your body is mine.

(He turns and leaves her alone. VIBHEESHANA, his brother, is waiting for him on the other side of the door)

VIBHEESH: Brother, this is part of some larger design! Whoever convinced you that you could steal Rama of Ayhoda's wife – wants you…wants all of us…Dead.

(RAVANA turns. VIBHEESHANA calls after him)

Ravana! RAVANA! *(But RAVANA walks away without turning back)*

XI.

(HANUMAN sits staring into the swelling tides of the ocean. An eagle spirals above him. It is DASARATHA, RAMA's father, who flies the eagle. In her cell, SITA stands. Her eyes are closed but she stretches her arms above her as though she sees the eagle in her dream. It lands near HANUMAN and speaks through DASARATHA)

DASARATHA as SAMPATI: Son of the Wind, what do you wait on the shores of doubt for?

HANUMAN: Great One. I would rather die than return to Rama with no news of the Devi.

DASARATHA as SAMPATI: She is prisoner to Ravana – Lord of the Rakshasas. He keeps her in in the City of Lanka, in his favourite Askovana.

HANUMAN: *(Astonished)* How do you know this?

DASARATHA as SAMPATI: My Brother, Jataya, died defending Sita. Go now, before it is too late. Her time is almost at an end.

HANUMAN: *(Desperately)* But how will I reach her? An ocean lies between me and Lanka.

SITA as SAMPATI: Why, Sun of the Wind, do you doubt yourself so much? *(Simply)* Jump!

HANUMAN: *(Laughing in disbelief)* Jump?
You regard me too highly, Great One.

SITA as SAMPATI: You have forgotten who you are, Vayuputra! As a child, you leapt into the sky because you thought the sun a succulent orange to devour! Indra flung a thunderbolt that merely grazed your cheek. When was it, Invincible One, that you became so afraid?

VALMIKI 1: Remembering ourselves on the long dust road – who among us would not rather forget and fold back into fear? But we are ever called to spread arms and free-fall into the fearless children we were once ordained to be.

(HANUMAN stands tall, as though the bonds of fear are falling from him like great chains coming apart. He roars)

HANUMAN: There was a time once, that I carried the moon in these hands around the earth. I could tear Lanka up by its roots if I wished – and bring Sita to Rama still on Lanka's soil. *(HANUMAN crouches and readies himself. Then roaring – he launches himself upwards into the sky)*

VALMIKI 2: Sitting on the shores of doubt – like dry wood waiting for kindling, the flame ignites. With a leap of faith, we are borne into the wind towards our true way.

4. Crossing Over

I.

(RAVANA's halls are silent – but for the breathing of slumber and the soporific swell of the ocean below. The plastic on the scaffolding billows and deflates. RAVANA twists in dreams, his magnificent dark form naked and laid with scars. MANDODARI sleeps soundly nearby. HANUMAN tiptoes through the halls. He stops and looks over the sleeping woman's face)

HANUMAN: *(Whispering)* Sita?

> *(MANDODARI stirs and mutters in her sleep. HANUMAN sees that though this woman's beauty fits RAMA's description, she is older than SITA could be)*

> *(He shrinks away as RAVANA groans softly and rises. HANUMAN follows RAVANA into the askovana, where he stands watching SITA sleep. He looks haunted and strangely vanquished. HANUMAN hides in the shadows. SITA sits up in fear)*

RAVANA: Rise from this cold, dust floor, and take your rightful place beside me as my Queen.

SITA: *(Looking him in the eyes)* Have you no one that cares for you here? Are they all too afraid to tell you: You will die Rakshasa! We are more than you will ever know.

RAVANA: It is known across the three worlds: I am invincible, my dear.

SITA: Are you?

RAVANA: Ten thousand years of perfect worship – for which Siva, God of Gods, granted me immortality…

SITA: Beware the man who believes he has God on his side.

RAVANA: No Deva, Danava, Daitya, Asura, Rakshasa, gandharva, kinnara, charana, siddha can touch me. Neither divine nor demonic beings can harm or end my life.

SITA: But in your arrogance, you forgot to ask invincibility from mortals, Rakshasa.

RAVANA: If I am immortal against the Devas – I assume *(he smiles)* this will protect me from your soft prince, who has known nothing but privilege all his life.

SITA: *(Looking deeply into his eyes)* Doom is coming to Lanka. You cannot imagine the love Rama enfolds me in. It will make of your city – ash. Do you not feel the shadows move this way?

(RAVANA smiles)

RAVANA: Are you trying to frighten the Lord of the Rakshasas?

SITA: I pity you.

RAMA: Save your pity. I am a brutal man.

SITA: You claim to have conquered thousands of women – yet you know nothing of our sex. Were I never promised to Rama, I would still rather die than give myself to you. No one has the courage to say it…but you are grotesque, Rakshasa.

Anyone…ANYONE could have me before you.

(RAVANA's fists are closing with rage – but SITA pushes on with great scorn)

When Rama's arrow is buried to its feathers in your Black heart – you will know how sad and impotent you truly are.

(For a long moment, RAVANA grows very still. In an instant he draws his sword and stands over her – weapon poised to decapitate her. SITA raises her face to his and gazes calmly into his eyes. They are locked in a silent struggle of wills. HANUMAN is about to reveal himself and intervene – but MANDODARI is suddenly behind RAVANA. She does not look at SITA. She wraps her arms around RAVANA's neck)

MANDODARI: The Harem is empty without you. I wait every night for you to come and enjoy new beauties captured but not yet tasted – from unknown realms. Our bodies burn for you. Come, husband, and let us take your anguish from you.

(RAVANA slowly backs away, though he does not take his eyes from SITA. Finally he allows himself to be led away. MANDODARI and SITA's

eyes briefly meet. MANDODARI nods and turns away. Alone, SITA sits quietly – drained. HANUMAN, remaining concealed lest he frighten SITA, begins to chant in Sanskrit, the narrative of RAMA and SITA's story. SITA stands stunned. SITA stands perfectly still. She closes her eyes and listens to her own history unfold. Gently, HANUMAN emerges from where he has been hiding and prostrates himself before her.

HANUMAN: Whose feet do I touch?

SITA: They call me Sita in this life.

HANUMAN: Devi – your Rama sent me to you.

SITA: *(Stunned)* My Rama?

(HANUMAN moves towards her in empathy. SITA shrinks from him and cries out)

If you are Ravana in another form…

(HANUMAN lays his face at her feet. SITA watches him for awhile, but he remains still. Slowly he holds a ring up to her)

Rama said to give you this ring that you would know he sent me…

(She tentatively takes it and looks at it. Tears flow when she finds it to be RAMA's. She falls to her knees)

SITA: Who are you?

HANUMAN: My people call me Hanuman, Devi.

(HANUMAN, with great humility, bows before her)

SITA: Forgive me for having doubted you, Hanuman. My faith has been worn thin. The Rakshasa will have me at all costs if I do not submit by full moon after next. I wait and pray. I don't know what more to do.

HANUMAN: You will not see another moon in Lanka, Devi.

SITA: But how will an entire army cross the ocean that lies between Rama and me?

HANUMAN: Be at peace, Devi…

SITA: The unthinkable had crossed my mind that Rama no longer…

(She can't go on)

HANUMAN: *(Quietly)* Before his eyes open each morning, he is uttering your name. Like a prayer. At night, "Sita" is his mantra over and under his tongue, until he sleeps.

(SITA sits on the bare earth and, for the first time, allows her grief to take its full force)

SITA: All this suffering is the karma of previous lives untold.

HANUMAN: Ravana will know his karma sooner than he can dream.

SITA: *(She turns to him. Her face is dark with thought)* Hanuman, I am a branch severed from my own life. Soon – I fear – I will be dead.

HANUMAN: Devi, I am the son of the wind. Climb on my back. I will cross the yawning sea and bring you to Rama this night!

SITA: *(Shaking her head gently but with immovable conviction)* Vayuputra, Ravana's powers reach father and deeper than we can imagine. Rama must come to Lanka to fight this dharma yuddha – and end Ravana's reign. What is my discomfort in the face of this holy war that must be fought time and time again?

HANUMAN: You are truly Rama of Ayhoda's wife.

SITA: *(But she is distracted)* Before the moon returns to the nakshatra he must come for me, Hanuman… Or we will never see each other in this lifetime again.

(HANUMAN looks at her, startled. He knows this is not said lightly)

HANUMAN: Devi, how might I prove to Rama that I saw you?

SITA: *(Her eyes fill with tears, though she smiles)* Speak to him of the time we were caught together in a sudden rain, and my tilaka was rubbed away. I lay my head in his lap when we found shelter in a cave. He took the dust of the mansila stone, kissed my brow gently and marked it. Then he spoke of the sons we would someday have. No one else could know about those hours we shared in that cavern alone. *(HANUMAN prostrates himself at SITA's feet. She blesses him. He stands)* I will not survive here beyond the next lunar month. I hope we meet again Vayuputra.

HANUMAN: Have no doubt, Devi. Before the moon returns to the nakshatra.

(HANUMAN bows deeply, turns and is gone)

SITA: *(Opening her palms and talking to RAMA as though he were present)* I have been lost my love. But dreamed of you last night. Your body on the timeless ocean, drifting toward me over great circles of pain. I came to you weeping.

You took my hand and we began to walk the dark waters. Even into the great sleep you were there – by my side.

(We see RAMA kneeling on the shore line beneath a full moon, facing Lanka. He rises and arches his back, giving his heart towards the light. With his eyes closed, he calls out her name)

II.

(RAVANA and his councilors surround HANUMAN – who is bound with ropes and curled on the floor. They turn him over. He gasps at the terrible beauty of RAVANA's ten heads)

HANUMAN: Ravana of Lanka, how magnificent you truly are.

RAMA: *(Locking eyes with HANUMAN, he hisses to VIBHEESHANA beside him)* Who is he? What does he want?

(The ten heads extend further from the neck in curiosity and smoldering rage)

HANUMAN: I am myself. In true form – a Vanara. No astra may bind me.

(He draws the ropes away from his body as though he were breaking fragile string)

I allowed myself to be captured because I wished to meet you face to faces. *(He smiles at his little joke)* Listen to my words and they may profit you – dark one.

(RAVANA says nothing but watches HANUMAN and waits)

She is the fire of truth you kindle. She will make of your city a wasteland of ash.

RAVANA: *(In a low growl)* Kill him.

VIBHEESHANA: My Lord – to kill the messenger is not dharma.

RAVANA: Have I not tolerated insults in a way that no King would?

VIBHEESHANA: Send an army against the human prince. A great warrior knows when not to strike. Let them say that Ravana spared the messanger's life –

(RAVANA's eyes flicker with rage – but the ten heads nod with calculation)

RAVANA: Set his tail alight, and then release him. I can think of no message more articulate for Rama than the burnt stump on your Vanara behind! BRING ME FIRE!

HANUMAN's tail is wrapped and dipped in oil.

As they touch fire to it – he turns to RAVANA.

HANUMAN: She is your death, magnificent one. And you will know it soon.

(HANUMAN leaps from where he stands – and with his tail blazing, tears through Lanka)

SITA: *(Stepping out of her current horror to reflect)* Hanuman lit the city of Lanka that night, as he ran across the roof tops, harvesting destruction wherever he went. He looked back once over his shoulder, jumped the ocean and with him – took my soul home

(KUSA and LAVA begin to sing, and we see HANUMAN beside RAMA once again, telling him all that occurred. He points across the sea into the distance. RAMA embraces HANUMAN fiercely and then stares out over the vast waters towards his love)

SITA: I stood amidst the flames of presence that night, beloved. I kept the heat at bay by inviting it in. But mothers and children burnt alive in their homes, where they had lain down to sleep in each other's arms. I will hold always in my heart, their unforgettable screams. Let us never forget: Pain is sown and harvested, my beloved, wherever the black boot of war goes.

III.

(RAMA sits on the shore in prayopavesha. LAKSHMANA sits beside him – also in prayer)

VALMIKI 1: With a singleness of thought we sit the silence and wait to cross the vast and ambitious sea of self.

(RAMA turns to LAKSHMANA)

RAMA: Bring me my bow.

(LAKSHMANA brings RAMA his bow. RAMA fits an arrow and then assuming alidha, he roars like an angry God)

If the gentle way will not be heard – I will open with force what remains closed to me here.

VALMIKI 1: The sky grows dark as Midnight. We stand like a flame upon the shore, as a great lament rises from the ocean, filled with ancient grief.

RAMA: VARUNA! I will consume you. I will make ash of your acres. Vast plains of desert with no memory that they once held water. I will cross into Lanka over your parched mountain ranges that sit now in dark waters below.

VALMIKI 2: The sun and moon stray from their orbits. Chaos verges on the inner world. And then the ocean recedes, as Varuna Deva – body of water and light – strides toward the shore.

(The Sea – SITA-BODY as water – prostrates itself at RAMA's feet)

SITA-BODY as VARUNA: Lord, it is the pristine and unbroken nature of the sun to shine; the wind to blow; the earth to turn. Not even I can still the waves that flow from me. Like you – I cannot be what I am not.

RAMA: You are in my way Varuna! And if I am ever to find my heart again – you must be crossed. I will decimate you and all life within you, if you do not give way.

VARUNA: I cannot be destroyed, Blue One. Find your way over my icy miles of fear and then I give you my word: As you and your untamed vanaras cross my waters...whatever way you find to achieve this – I will hold you in my arms.

(The sound of grief becomes the breath of the ocean once more)

SUGRIVA: Shall we begin, my Lord?

RAMA: Begin...?

SUGRIVA: The work. The sacred bridge we must build across these waves to bring us to Lanka.

RAMA: How is this possible, Sugriva?

SUGRIVA: We are a magical people, Lord. The vanaras have ranged the earth since the beginning of time. There is much work to be done...

(RAMA nods silently like a child and drops to his knees. SUGRIVA gives an ancient war cry, calling the Vanaras to begin their sacred task)

IV.

(RAVANA moves through the ashes of Lanka. Everywhere, HANUMAN has left destruction in his wake. RAVANA faces the audience – amongst whom sits INDRAJIT his son; VIBHEESHANA his brother and councilors. He addresses the audience as though addressing his own Senate. MANDODARI stands silently nearby)

RAVANA: *(He pauses to gather his power and then looks directly at his senate)* I come to you for council, for we will soon be at war. Are we ready to show The Blue Prince and his Monkeys that we intend to rule for another age?

(The room echos with the roars of the RAKSHASAS. Suddenly a lone voice speaks)

VIBHEESHANA: My brother, hear me! I alone love you in this sabha. For I alone will tell you the truth: Return Sita at Rama's side, or we are all doomed.

(Turning to the council of RAKSHASAS, RAVANA roars)

RAVANA: I am Ravana of Lanka. My valour is as deep as the ocean. I am as strong as Vayu. Do I look doomed to you?

(The RAKSHASAS roar in response)

VIBHEESHANA: You hunger as a man – yet will destroy like a child – whatever stands in the way of making Rama's wife your queen.

(RAVANA turns with blazing eyes to his brother. All look to MANDODARI, but she keeps her face blank, as inscrutable as ever)

The price has already been considerable! Rama's Monkey has left our city in ash. An army of Vanaras are headed towards our gates. Your woman troubles will end us all!

INDRAJIT: How dare you?

VIBHEESHANA: I say this not to humiliate you, brother. But to prevent your untimely death.

INDRAJIT: Rama of Ayhoda is not a god but a man. The weakest among us could kill this mortal prince.

(VIBHEESHANA smiles with patronizing but genuine pity at INDRAJIT)

VIBHEESHANA: You are young, Meghanada – and though you are already a legend on the battle field – you should not be here amongst your elders. You are yet a boy.

(Blazing with rage, INDRAJIT opens his mouth to retaliate – but VIBHEESHANA simply turns from him, back to RAVANA)

Return Sita to her husband's side and beg on broken knees before The Blue Prince. Then come home in peace to Lanka, and rule for another age. Ask forgiveness from Rama of Ayhoda or Lanka is surely doomed.

RAVANA: *(RAVANA turns to his brother, smiling and eyes burning with rage)* Never.

(Everyone roars with approval)

VIBHEESHANA: *(Turning to the Senate)* Show him your love, Rakshasas, by stopping him. Use any means necessary. He cannot save his own life.

RAVANA: *(In a terrifying rage)* You are an enemy to Lanka from this day forward.

VIBHEESHANA: These very Rakshasas who urge you forward today will soon be silenced.
Their brave bodies, rotting flesh for scavenger birds by tomorrow's setting sun.

(His eyes glistening with tears)

Forgive me, brother. I wanted only to save your life.
We will not meet in peace in this lifetime again.

(VIBHEESHANA rises and walks out of the assembly – leaving the council in stunned silence)

V.

VALMIKI 1: Finally we must all traverse the bridge between what we know and where we have no choice but to go.

(RAMA stands on the completed bridge the Vanaras built. He makes a ritual blessing. They look up into the distance, and along the bridge from Lanka – comes VIBHEESHANA. He prostrates himself before him)

RAMA: Who is at my feet?

VIBHEESHANA: Brother to Ravana of Lanka.

(LAKSHMANA and SUGRIVA look to one another stunned, hands on their weapons. HANUMAN recalls VIBHEESHANA from his night in Lanka and stands, quietly observing him)

I am branded a traitor and banished, my Lord.

LAKSHMANA: *(With his weapon in hand)* Why?

VIBHEESHANA: I will not lie to you, Rama of Ayhoda. I love my brother. I wanted to save his life. But he would not hear my pleas to return Sita to your side.

LAKSHMANA: Do you come alone?

VIBHEESHANA: I have abandoned even my wives and children in Lanka – though I know they are doomed. I come to serve in whatever way I can.

SUGRIVA: We cannot risk this.

(RAMA looks at LAKSHMANA)

LAKSHMANA: I wait your decision. If you declare him friend, I will embrace him with my heart. Name him Enemy – and I will kill him without a moment's pause.

RAMA: *(Looking to HANUMAN who waits quietly)* Hanuman?

HANUMAN: *(Quietly)* Vibheeshana spoke for my life in Ravana's sabha when death was certain. He has chosen the way of the dharma over his own flesh and blood. What further proof could be asked but the abandonment of all he loves?

SUGRIVA: This is a Rakshasa, Lord Rama. Lying is their way. Betrayal – their song.

VIBHEESHANA: *(Prostrating himself at Rama's feet again)* My life is yours.

(All wait to know VIBHEESHANA's fate)

RAMA: The way of the dharma is clear on this: No one who seeks sanctuary should ever be turned away.

(He lays his hand gently on the Rakshasa's head. VIBHEESHANA begins to weep)

You are embraced as brother to us all.

(RAMA helps him rise. LAKSHMANA, SUGRIVA and HANUMAN unreservedly each embrace VIBHEESHANA in turn)

RAMA: *(To LAKSHMANA)* Bring us water from the sea. We will crown this brother King of the Rakshasas. Those who survive what is coming to Lanka, will need someone to rule.

(LAKSHMANA gathers water from the shore. RAMA anoints VIBHEESHANA. They stand on the bridge, looking across the waters as daylight begins to fade)

Tomorrow, brave Vanaras and Rakshasas will lie dead side by side – their lives extinguished on Lanka's shores. Their blood will colour the earth. And my heart breaks for us all.

(The women around the SITA-BODY stretch her out once more, and one by one, they kiss her brow and sing of loss and war. LAKSHMANA,

RAMA, VIBHEESHANA, SUGRIVA and HANUMAN walk away on the windswept beach, as VIBHEESHANA shares the secrets of Lanka)

VIBHEESHANA: Like your native Ayhoda – there are Nine Gates by which one can breach our city wall…

VALMIKI 2: Nine points of entry. As it always was, and will be, in matters of the heart.

(The women gathered around the SITA-BODY, massage the heart area and turn her onto her side)

VI.

(SITA sits in her cell – fervently chanting the Vedas. In his chamber, RAVANA is woken by INDRAJIT)

INDRAJIT: Father, wake up! Rama and his monkeys have reached our shores.

RAVANA: Impossible.

INDRAJIT: They will soon be at the city gates. Your Rakshasas wait to hear from you.

(RAVANA rises with urgency disguised as fury and moves to the window to address his RAKSHASAS below)

RAVANA: You dare stand before me – trembling like virgins in my Harem!
(Roaring) HAVE YOU FORGOTTEN WHO WE ARE?
(The RAKSHASAS roar)

RAMA: *(Suddenly from the Northern Gate)* You could have been King of the Devas! It is YOU, Rakshasa, who has forgotten who you are!

(RAVANA looks out into the early morning to see RAMA standing on the wall. At last they face each other)

You offered the world a gift when you stole my wife. For now Rama of Ayhoda is at your city gates, and the hour of retribution is come. Return Sita to me; and save countless lives.

(The VALMIKIS are at the feet and head of the SITA-BODY. They will both offer accounts of what comes next, using the body like a map, a land on which the war will ensue. They will mark it with diagrams, write words on it, run their hands over it. The SITA-BODY is lit to look like the undulating hills and plains of Lanka)

VALMIKI 2: Countless Rakshasas – armed to the teeth – stare out at an ocean of Vanaras, waiting to storm their nine gates.

RAMA: What do you say Ravana? There is yet time to turn this around.

(RAVANA smiles)

RAVANA: *(Smiling)* No wonder she loves you, beautiful Rama. Your heart shines like time.

VALMIKI 1: Rama turns to his monkey men and simply nods. The roar is deafening as vanaras surge forward, each monkey determined to be the first over Lanka's walls.

(The VALMIKIS use the SITA-BODY to tell the story of the coming war. The powerful song of LAVA and KUSA, and the singing from the VALMIKIS at the SITA-BODY, alternately score the war narrative throughout)

VALMIKI 2: What mathematics of time and fate have brought each warrior to this battlefield to face Yamma's gates? Only the gods know and they are silent, as blood flows and the plan follows its invisible design.

VALMIKI 1: Tar black blood glistens on Lanka's fields like dark dew. The Rakshasas are ferocious but Sugriva's monkey brethren plough through exhaustion and cry out with renewed strength under the rising moon.

(RAMA and LAKSHMANA stand centre, side by side – releasing their bows with awe-inspiring prowess)

VALMIKI 2: Not an arrow of Rama and Lakshmana's fails to claim a Rakshasa life. After 13 hours of relentless battle, the Rakshasas flee the mighty Vanara storm.

VII.

(RAVANA sits hissing on his throne like a serpent. Even his own ministers cannot bear the sight of him. INDRAJIT enters and approaches his father)

INDRAJIT: Take some wine, father. And some women for the night. Let history smile through the ages, that when the Vanaras came to Lanka's gates, the Great Ravana did not get to his feet. His son took care of The Blue Prince alone.

(INDRAJIT turns swiftly and in a deft move, is out onto the battle field. The Rakshasas roar: Jaya Indrajit! Jaya!)

VALMIKI 2: Indrajit was born with war in his veins. Preparation for battle was an experience never matched for him by any women. At the edge of the field now, he kindles a fire and worships the Navagraha, the nine planets, the sacred fire.

(INDRAJIT performs his legendary Yagna in preparation for battle. He chants mantras. When the ceremony is concluded, he speaks to his gods)

INDRAJIT: I am Indrajit, who conquered the king of the Devas! Bring me Rama of Ayhoda. And his pale brother. In my father's name – I will have them both.

VALMIKI 1: In a deadly battle for their Yuvaraja, the Vanaras fight with ferocity. But Lanka's son brings the ancient craft of "Maya" to those death fields today.

VALMIKI 2: Filling the skies with visions so exquisite, the monkeys cannot tear their eyes from the beauty of death as it falls like deadly rain.

RAMA: *(To LAKSHMANA at his side, watching the extraordinary weapons of Maya)* It is Brahma's mysteries he invokes. He wants us to run in fear. He does not know whom he faces today.

VALMIKI 1: Whispering – the fiery blossoms gently tumble towards the monkey army, whose faces are turned up in awe like children watching the monsoon storms. And one by one, every monkey falls into the halls of waiting, where only Yamma calls.

RAMA: *(Calling out to LAKSHMANA)* They are held in the blossoms' deadly power. Call the brahmana's trance away from the forest people to us. Against it – only we may stand a chance.

(RAMA and LAKSHMANA draw the deadly blossom towards themselves and fall deep into coma. In the dense darkness that has fallen – we hear a beautiful chanting. The only thing visible is the SITA-BODY – though covered in the marks of war – shining with incandescent light)

VALMIKI 1: Dreams of Brahmaloka draw the brothers far from the bloodied fields of Lanka, and into realms they must forget when they wake… If they ever do. For the torpor of the brahmastra is said to last until the universe vanishes in the pralaya. And then everything must, painstakingly, atom by atom, begin once again.

(A match is lit. VIBHEESHANA stands holding out a small flame. A lone torch slowly weaves its way towards him. He sees it is HANUMAN approaching. They embrace fiercely)

VIBHEESH: Brahma truly blessed you that his own powers are useless against you!

HANUMAN: *(Falling to his knees when he sees his Lord and brother lying unconscious at his feet)* RAMA! LAKSHMANA!

VIBHEESH: Do not despair, Hanuman! The Prince's are beneath death's mountain – but not yet dead.

HANUMAN: Lost in Brahmaloka! How will we ever bring them back?

VIBHEESH: As long as Hanuman lives – there is hope!

HANUMAN: *(Looking at VIBHEESHANA incredulously)* Brother. What good is my body's strength, in the search for Rama – lost in the void from which no living thing returns?

VIBHEESH: Son of the Wind – it was never muscle and sinew alone that enabled you: It is what you are willing to give that saved us before and will save us now. Fly again for us, Heart of Devotion, across the ocean. Only you can save the Princes of Khosala and our fallen army.

HANUMAN: To where can I fly? I am lost.

VIBHEESHANA: In the north range of the Himalayas, miraculous plants of healing grow on the slopes of Oshadhiparvata. You will know the herbs by the soft light they shine with after dark. FLY Hanuman – and bring back these oshadis. With them I will raise our army from death's waiting chamber. I will be in the black night amongst our fallen, counting the hours until your return.

(HANUMAN opens his arms wide, exposing the heart area of his chest. He rises and flies into the night)

5. Darkness

I.

(INDRAJIT sweeps into the cell where SITA sits chanting the vedas. She stops when he enters. It is the first time he has seen her. He is rocked to the core by her beauty. He reaches out slowly and runs a finger along her jaw and brow, down her neck – stopping short of going further)

INDRAJIT: They did not lie. You are exquisite, Sita of Rama! I would have you myself...
But here in Lanka, we let our father's eat first, and are happy to suck like scavengers on bones, once our elders lie sated.

(SITA tries to cover herself, terrified. Whereas RAVANA is deeply in love with SITA, INDRAJIT emanates only pure, carnal lust. She turns away, chanting. INDRAJIT pulls RAMA's bow from behind his back and casts it in front of her. SITA looks up, frantically searching INDRAJIT's face)

SITA: Where did you get this? Rama would never let you take it alive.

INDRAJIT: Exactly, beautiful one. I have felled Rama and his brother last night as a woodman might two young saplings.

SITA: I dreamt this.

INDRAJIT: Dead.

SITA: No...

INDRAJIT: Dead enough, sweet one. In a slumber that the gods themselves could not rise from – let alone two mortal men.

SITA: *(Turning inwards, whispering desperately into cupped hands)* Is it true my love? Are you gone from this realm? The silken threads that hold us bound begin to strain. Are you still with me Rama?

(RAVANA is suddenly behind INDRAJIT, who immediately steps away in deference)

RAVANA: You have eyes that see through time, Sita. You know he speaks the truth.

(SITA begins to rock herself, moaning – grief coming in vast waves)

SITA: Rama, beloved. I feel breath but no heart beat. Heart beat but no breath. What if in the mountains of ages I must climb… I never find you again?

RAVANA: All your punya and your vratas could not protect them. Rise and ready yourself to be Queen!

SITA: *(Rocking, and whispering to RAMA between vedas)* Into the chambers of your beating heart – I breathe life, Blue Prince. Lakshmana, wherever you both may be, find the portal back to this realm.

INDRAJIT: *(Grabbing her brutally by the hair and screaming into her face)* The sands of our northern beaches are dark with monkey blood and faeces of fear. Your hermit boy is DEAD, whore!

(RAVANA, with one powerful and startling blow, strikes INDRAJIT from SITA. He reels – from shock rather than the pain – for he is more than RAVANA's equal in strength. But father and son have never been at odds before)

RAVANA: She is my Queen. Mother to you soon. Touch her again or speak to her that way… And you will die by this hand that once held yours as a boy.

(INDRAJIT staggers back staring at RAVANA and SITA, his eyes stinging with tears. He turns and is gone. MANDODARI has been watching from the shadows. She steps in and looks deeply at SITA)

RAVANA: You do not have my leave to be here, woman.

SITA: Who are you?

MANDODARI: *(She is overcome at the sight of SITA, but gathers herself seamlessly)* You are beautiful, Sita.
And brave and true.
I understand now why he is willing to lose his kingdom, the love of his favourite son, his Queen…
For you –

(She reaches out and pulls the devastated SITA towards her)

Leave her with me, Ravana. I will calm her as the women of your harem once calmed me. *(To SITA)* Rest awhile child. You are safe for now, in my arms.

(She strokes SITA's hair. In her grief, SITA surrenders to this feminine, gentle touch. MANDODARI holds her against her breast rocking her, as she weeps. RAVANA watches them, curiously moved. He backs away, – leaving his Queen with the great love of his life. Once alone, MANDODARI's face is still but she silently weeps)

II.

VALMIKI 1: As evening falls, Hanuman sees the Himalayas ahead of him. The slopes of the smallest peak glow with other worldly light. Hanuman grasps Oshadhiarvata by its sides, and tears that mountain's roots out of the earth. Body blazing, he does not stop until he reaches Rama's silent body in Lanka and places the mountain at his side.

(A mound of earth is placed on the belly of the SITA-BODY. A magnificent creature, GARUDA – half eagle, half man – circles above the unconscious RAMA)

VALMIKI 1: In the weighty sleep of Nagpasa, Rama wonders: Is it my soul circling above – as it has done when it finally left the body in countless previous lives? I see my mother's eyes and long for her cool touch on the back of my neck when I was a boy. I feel my father near. His dark eyes looking for me when I would disappear into the shadowed gardens of home as a child. Is it you, father – come to call us back into the deep?

(GARUDA comes in for landing. DASARATHA flies him and speaks for him. He assumes a human form as he lands on earth – a manly physique – though his head is an eagle's and his wings are folded behind him)

GARUDA: I am Garuda – your witness through the aeons. I can appear to you but once in each span of life. I bring word that neither the Devas nor gandharvas can lift the slumber in which you are bound. But Hanuman brings a mountain of devotion to your side. Fear nothing Future King. Ramaraja is soon here.

(RAMA and LAKSHMANA rise to their feet and watch the eagle circle and soar away)

(RAVANA hears the cry of the eagle over the night's silence)

RAVANA: *(To himself)* It is not possible Dasartha's sons rise again! *(Roaring)* Send every son I have to go among the legions. BRING ME THE KOSALA BROTHERS' HEARTS!

VALMIKI 2: The Rakshasas run full force towards the battle fields – fearless to pay with their lives. But the Vanaras have seen Rama rise from nagpasa tonight. They fight with joyous ferocity. Every Rakshasa, every son of Ravana's… falls.

(RAVANA stands in perfect stillness – his ten heads out in full rage)

RAVANA: *(Fiercely)* Ready me for battle! It is time.

III.

(RAMA is watching the Rakshasas sweep into battle from a distance. Suddenly he sees RAVANA's awesome figure in their midsts. He turns to VIBHEESHANA)

RAMA: Vibheeshana: The dust and heat blind me – but I feel a new pulse among us. Is it He that now leads the Rakshasas to the field?

VIBHEESHANA: *(Unable to hide his pride)* It is He, my lord – Lord of them All. The dark beating heart at the centre – is always my brother.

RAMA: *(Turning to VIBHEESHANA gently with a smile)* You love him. More fiercely than ever.

(VIBHEESHANA looks away in shame. RAMA looks back at the advancing demon army. He watches RAVANA)

(In a low voice to VIBHEESHANA, with great respect)

How magnificent he truly is. If ever there was one who could have been King of the Devas…

VIBHEESHANA: But he took the way of the night, the left path of the soul and he must be stopped.

Never doubt me Rama. When the time comes, I will kill him with my own hands, if you ask.

(RAMA embraces VIBHEESHANA, who receives the strength, pulls away and nods at RAMA – who nods in return)

VALMIKI 2: The Rakshasa King wades through the monkey men – severing limbs and torsos with terrifying ease. Sugriva heaves any rock, stone or tree he can uproot and hurl – destroying every arrow in flight. But Ravana finds his mark…

VALMIKI 1: The serpent astra buries itself in the Monkey King's breast.

(SUGRIVA falls on the blood-soaked earth)

VALMIKI 2: Monkey arms, legs, heads lie strewn at his feet. Ravana's archery is an ancient prowess of warriors born of another age and time.

(HANUMAN, in rage at the death of his kinsmen, charges at RAVANA)

HANUMAN: Rakshasa, you have Brahma's blessing but no protection against this monkey fist of mine.

RAVANA: Come monkey fist. Kill me if you can.

HANUMAN: Have you forgotten how I ended each of your sons yesterday?

(Enraged, RAVANA strikes at HANUMAN's chest, knocking the great Vanara to the ground. He staggers to his feet and shakes off the extraordinary force of the blow. He strikes suddenly, at the stunned demon king)

RAVANA: *(RAVANA reels from the blow. Recovering quickly, though shaken now)* Well done, monkey fist! More power than I thought.

VALMIKI 2: A shadow falls silently onto the battlefield now. Every Rakshasa, terrified, turns and flees.

RAVANA: From what do you dare run?

(When he looks back – it is to the awesome sight of LAKSHMANA standing utterly still – watching him. They lock eyes)

Foolish human! Prepare to pass through Yama's gates!

LAKSHMANA: I wait for you, old man. Will we talk? Or will we fight?

(RAVANA raises his bow)

VALMIKI 1: Ravana's fiery missiles race towards Lakshmana. The kshatriya moves faster than the eye can hold. In moments, the shafts fall tamely around him – serpents without heads.

(RAVANA shouts out his admiration)

Lakshmana sends a volley that cleaves, in two, the bow in Ravana's hand.

(RAVANA stands stunned, as blood blooms all over his awesome physique)

VALMIKI 2: His bow in pieces, Ravana is hurt often and grievously. He invokes Brahma's feminine power and hurls it at Lakshmana. The small, deadly sun takes LAKSHMANA centre of the chest.

(LAKSHMANA is instantly rendered unconscious. RAVANA tries to take LAKSHMANA's body from the battlefield, but he cannot lift his weight)

RAVANA: How is it that I, who once tore Mount Kailasa up by the roots, cannot move this human with all my strength?

HANUMAN: *(HANUMAN roars at the RAKSHASA, giving him a vicious blow. RAVANA falls, stunned)* The man you try to raise carries Rama's Dharma. You will never carry such holy burden, Rakshasa. Who can carry such weight?

(RAVANA, bleeding from the mouth, stumbles backwards to a sitting position. HANUMAN lifts and carries LAKSHMANA to RAMA and places his silent body at RAMA's feet. RAMA falls to his knees and touches LAKSHMANA with great love)

RAMA: When we sat as boys watching the monsoons in silence, I saw this moment once. You asked what I smiled at then. I was silent but I saw you rise from the grasp of brahmashakti. I have seen you by my side always, into the dark cave of time. Wake brother. Open your eyes.

(LAKSHMANA opens his eyes and smiles when he sees RAMA)

VALMIKI 2: Ravana moves through the monkey-men like death. Countless vanaras fall in the wake of his fury. Their screams fill the blue Lankan skies.

(An unearthly sound rings out)

VALMIKI 1: But a single note from Rama's bow silences all.

RAMA: Ravana, prepare for your end. Siva himself cannot offer you sanctuary from me.

VALMIKI 1: The Blue One fights with the wisdom of the Fathers through age and time.
Ravana has no answer to the Blue One's archery.
When Ravana is on his knees like a boy, Rama prepares a final shaft –
But drops his bow…

RAMA: *(With a smile)* Go home, Old Man.

RAVANA: *(Devastated by this humiliation, he screams)* Lift your bow!

RAMA: My dharma is to kill the great Ravana. Not an old man on his knees. Go home.
Return tomorrow an opponent worthy of me.

RAVANA: *(He staggers backwards)* More savage is your "kindness" than any fire you bring.

(With profound humiliation, he leaves the battlefield)

IV.

(SITA is in her confinement, still chanting vedas. Shafts of light suggest the setting of sun as she prays and waits. RAVANA sits on his throne – a broken version of himself. He has aged ten-fold since this all began. INDRAJIT stands before his father RAVANA. MANDODARI watches from nearby)

INDRAJIT: To see my father, the mighty Ravana, broken like a woman… Rise and claim yourself, King of Lanka.

RAVANA: *(Almost in a trance)* A yuga ago, I once ravished a chaste woman, Vedavati – and she cursed me. Perhaps Sita is Vedavati… Born again to be my death.

(INDRAJIT strides towards his father, yelling with disgust and rage)

INDRAJIT: WE ARE DYING OUT THERE IN THE THOUSANDS! FOR YOU!

(RAVANA pays no attention to INDRAJIT's tirade. He turns to the silent MANDODARI)

RAVANA: I feel I know her…from another time…

INDRAJIT: *(Desperate)* What does Ravana want his favourite son to do?

RAVANA: *(Becoming suddenly lucid and focused)* Bring me Rama of Ayhoda's heart by any means.

INDRAJIT: Any?

RAVANA: But do not harm Her in any way.

(INDRAJIT touches his father's feet. As he stands)

INDRAJIT: I will fight for you, father.
But I will never forgive you for loving her more than you do me.

(He turns and leaves his father slumped in the chair hiding his face behind his hand; and his mother watching quietly from the corner)

V.

VALMIKI 1: Hanuman leads the storming vanaras into battle. But what he sees coming is a sight none could have dreamed.

HANUMAN: STOP! Do not throw a single stone or tree.

(In INDRAJIT's arms is SITA-BODY)

HANUMAN: Fetch Rama!

INDRAJIT: *(Grabbing her by her hair)* Is this what you come looking for?

(Between the two armies, in front of every vanara and rakshasa – INDRAJIT grabs the SITA-BODY and kisses her violently. He strikes out and he slaps her face with such force that everyone present is stunned)

HANUMAN: Rakshasa! You do not dare. For this you will die.

INDRAJIT: She has stolen my father's soul. I will speak for each Rakshasa life lost over this whore!

HANUMAN: Even you would not break Dharma like this, Rakshasa!

INDRAJIT: You speak of dharma, Vanara! How many women and their children perished the night you turned our city to ash? You of Rama's forces claim righteousness. But in war – it is ALWAYS the innocent who die.

(Everyone is quiet)

(In one move, INDRAJIT snaps the SITA-BODY's neck. HANUMAN and the vanaras are stunned, motionless. None can believe what INDRAJIT has done)

INDRAJIT: Tell Rama of Ayhoda his whore is dead.

(SITA stands in the shadows watching. She sings softly to herself)

VI.

(RAMA stands to welcome HANUMAN as he appears, but stops short, seeing his grief)

HANUMAN: Indrajit brought Sita to the battlefield.

(RAMA stands quietly, waiting for the fatal blow to fall on his heart)

RAMA: And… *(Losing control)* …SPEAK!

HANUMAN: …Broke her gentle neck.

(RAMA opens his mouth, but no sound will come. He falls to his knees. LAKSHMANA, still extremely fragile from his earlier injury, turns and grabs RAMA by the shoulders)

LAKSHMANA: *(Filled with bitter rage)* Stand brother! The hour is come.

(But RAMA is beyond hearing or speech)

Brother – rise up and follow your Dharma. It is time for the Rakshasa King and his son to die!

(RAMA gasps for air)

LAKSHMANA: Will you let him defeat you in grief? Rise brother. Now is the time to honour what he has destroyed. Rama on his knees weeping – is what he was hoping for.

VIBHEESHANA: *(Without emotion)* Where is her body?

HANUMAN: Indrajit left with it.

VIBHEESHANA: Ravana loves Sita more than his kingdom, more than his own life. He would never let Indrajit or any...

(Suddenly he understands what INDRAJIT is doing)

O dear god! Rise! We must hurry to Nikumbhila! It was a Maya Sita that Indrajit created.

HANUMAN: *(Trying to grasp what is being said)* A Maya Sita ?

VIBHEESHANA: A body in her likeness conjured from the mysteries of the parallel world. I have once seen him dabble such sorcery in the past. It is his cunning to shock us into grief that he may win crucial time.

HANUMAN: Time for what?

VIBHEESHANA: Indrajit is sitting yagna at this moment - to make himself invincible. If we do not stop him...All is lost!

(Turning grimly to LAKSHMANA, his face still pale – his eyes dark, he lays his hands on LAKSHMANA's bowed head. He is still unable to speak)

LAKSHMANA: Bless me, my brother and my God. The hour of my life's purpose has come.

VII.

(INDRAJIT sits before a fire, his lean scarred body bare. He feeds the fire with ghee. Like a fierce priest, he is absorbed in his sacrifice, chanting mantras of power. VIBHEESHANA throws a stone nearby. Hearing the noise, INDRAJIT rises and comes to see who is there. Seeing his uncle, he is enraged)

INDRAJIT: May you be damned forever for showing them our sacred Nikumbhila! We will never again speak your name in Lanka. For you betray your bretheren. And nothing is lower. *(He spits)*

VIBHEESHANA: You may be a great warrior, child. But were you to survive the ages – you will never have the truth of the Fathers. In this, you will always be a boy.

INDRAJIT: You are a traitor. No matter what I have done – I will not have sold my own.

VIBHEESHANA: It is over, son.

INDRAJIT: *(Smiling strangely)* Indeed. I have sat the fire and the war is now won.

VIBHEESHANA: But did you finish sitting yagna? Can you be sure?

(VIBHEESHANA sharply meets his eye. There is fear in him now)

Or whilst you have been speaking bold words with me… Is Rama's brother not sitting comfortably at your fire. I believe the sacred blessing is now irretrievably his!

(He turns to see LAKSHMANA seated at his yagna fire. INDRAJIT freezes)

VALMIKI 2: For the first moment in his savage life – Indrajit is afraid.

(The fight is on)

Only the greatest archers, instructed by the most knowing gurus could match brother to Rama with Lanka's fiercest son.

VALMIKI 1: Into such battles, we meet our equal and find that we are battling our shadow:

The one that whispers to us of ourselves.

LAKSHMANA: *(In fierce prayer, drawing the bow)* If the Ishvaku Line have always honoured their word – let this moment be Indrajit's last.

(He launches an arrow. When the blinding light of the astra fades, LAKSHMANA stands covered in INDRAJIT's blood. Of INDRAJIT's body nothing remains)

VIII.

(RAVANA is on his knees, roaring at the news of the death of his son. MANDODARI stands, fist over mouth, nearby. RAVANA rises like a tidal wave and moves to the cell where SITA is kept. She is standing as he enters, ready for him – fire raging in her eyes)

RAVANA: My sons are dead and Lanka lies in ruins.

(SITA matches his stare)

SITA: You can kill me – but you will not have me.
　　You can take me but I will not be yours.
　　In this life time and all those to come – I will never love you.
　　Take my life, Rakshasa!
　　I am ready – to die.

RAVANA: It is not your life I come for.

(He is moving towards her with resolve and intent)

I hear your wings beating against the broken window of my
hatred. We will drown together, Daughter of Janaka. Like you
– I am not afraid to die.

SITA: What will this profit you? The battle is lost.

RAVANA: Your Rama has one fatal flaw. He is a man. And though
he will despise himself for it – he will never want you again.
For I know best of all: The battle of the self is the hardest won
of any war.

SITA: You give up everything for this?

RAVANA: Our destinies will die together, Child of the Dharma.

*(He moves to the SITA-BODY. He tears the clothes from it and rapes it
with pure violence. SITA stands at some distance, quietly watching as
the SITA-BODY takes the force. He looks up to find SITA staring deeply
into his eyes)*

Don't look at me!

(Roaring) LOOK AWAY!

(But she stares at him unflinchingly – for the duration of the rape)

*(RAVANANA stands. He looks now only at the SITA-BODY curled in a
foetal position on the floor. He backs out and away)*

VALMIKI 1: Essence and Body wait – like sisters – to float back in
to one another after the storm.

*(MANDODARI steps out of the shadows. She gathers the broken
and bleeding SITA-BODY into her arms. They are both weeping.*

MANDODARI begins to sing her an ancient lullaby. SITA watches from nearby. She sings too)

MANDODARI: History has been kind to me. Called me faithful and true. But when I saw what kind of devotion he was capable of after all...

(RAVANA walks onto the battlefield alone. His arms open wide, he shows he is unarmed. The boys KUSA and LAVA sing in their haunting pitch as RAMA approaches. LAKSHMANA has a weapon poised and HANUMAN stands some distance away – ready for an attack from the Lord of the Rakshasas. RAVANA looks deeply into RAMA's eyes)

RAMA: What makes you weep, Rakshasa? What makes you smile?

RAVANA: My sons are dead, my city in ashes, my harem empty, my legions slain.
I kneel before you – as naked as a newborn.

RAMA: On broken knees... but I smell no shame.

RAVANA: *(Shrugging)* This war has been fought in ages gone. It will be fought again and again. Our story will never end.

RAMA: I will find you as the tide rises in every age. We will face each other always with you on broken knees.

RAVANA: And you will lose her in every lifetime – as you do today.

RAMA: Sita lives.

RAVANA: In me and I in her.

(RAMA stands back startled, though he retains his poise of certainty)

I am sated finally. I believe she feels the same.

(RAMA stands perfectly still for several long moments, searching for the truth in RAVANA's eyes. RAMA lifts his sword, his hand shaking with tension about to be released by his rage. But he stops to see a woman enter the battlefield. It is MANDODARI. She comes to her husband who is moments from death)

RAVANA: *(Not taking his eyes from RAMA, he tells MANDODARI)* Go home.

MANDODARI: I will speak.

RAVANA: *(Ferociously)* WOMAN! GO HOME!

RAMA: *(Sensing the power of her intention)* Speak...

MANDODARI: *(To RAVANA)* Love of my life: I have a tale to tell. And it will be the last thing you live to hear: A tale designed a thousand leagues below an ocean – dark through the ages – where nothing will ever shine. I take it upon my shoulders. A stone that will bring me no peace but, at last, makes my suffering real. Mine is a tale of she whose name was Mandodari in this life. A great queen. Her husband tore her from her mother when she was still a child, and shaped her to his desires... Grew her to his tastes – like a plant turned downwards from the sun. Her husband was a great Rakshasa. Perhaps the greatest ever lived. He held the three realms: Swarga, Bhumi and Patala with ease in a single hand. Yet Mandodari's life was a desert of nothing but desire and shame. Not a night passed that she did not lay hungering for her king. Hating yet hungering – she slowly drew away from the light until she knew nothing outside of him alone. He came for her less and less as his harem grew. She thought perhaps some day he would be satiated with the endless new bodies open to him. But as he consumed – so his hunger over the years – grew. Yearning for the urgency of his battle-scarred body, time passed as a daily eternity, yet spilled extravagantly through her fingers as years. Her leaves turned gold and then grey and floated away.

RAVANA: I never stopped...

MANDODARI: *(Raising a hand to silence him)* One night she woke alone again. As she lay watching the moonlight shift across the walls of her cell, she knew that at last she hated him more than she needed him to come for her. She wanted suddenly to see him suffer as she had all these years. And there came a day when she knew she had the means. For, though she had told nobody – Mandodari was with child. And she was certain that growing in her was, at last, a girl: The daughter that Ravana had longed for more than anything else. Here, finally, was something she could take instead of give. And she sang to the pain and joy growing in her womb. She hid the swelling planes of her body from all – merely sent a message to her husband that she wished to go on pilgrimage to the Holy Trithas. He agreed, though he did not come and say goodbye. Perhaps that was the last possibility that their fates could have shifted. But he stayed away. She hardened her heart for what lay ahead.

(RAVANA turns from where he is kneeling, to stare at MANDODARI – struck dumb by what she is unravelling before him)

Mandodari knew the child in her womb was no ordinary life. The wife of Ravana knew peace in those months for the first time in her life. Away from Lanka, her body growing heavier each day – she carried a peace borne of the promise of coming revenge. And for once – the burning was still. In her ninth month, she mounted a stallion and rode dazed and utterly alone through the world until she felt the first savage tug in her womb. She drifted between sleep and wakefulness on the forest's edge. For hours, she lay in her body of sorrow and wept for the child she would never know. At dawn, she rose and managed a few steps toward the nearby city, before her birth waters broke. Squatting down in a field alone, she pushed life from her and held in her arms a golden baby girl. Never had she known what she felt as she held the child for that short hour. Her daughter's eyes watching up at her with their ancient questions, the small mouth waiting for her mother's breast. But vengeance was the only thing that would make life in Lanka bearable for Mandodari in her remaining years. With a last kiss – she laid the child down on the earth, buried her birth sack and umbilical chord close by, climbed her black steed and rode back to Lanka alone. As dawn broke – it is told – Janaka of Mathila moved through the morning light, towards a field on the southern outskirts of his land. With his golden plough, he wanted to turn the earth for a sacrifice that morning.

(RAVANA begins to moan like a beast)

And there in a furrow of the earth he found a baby girl.

RAVANA: NO…No please no…

MANDODARI: He named her Sita. Took her home and raised her as his own. That body you have loved, used, broken. She is your only daughter. Your own flesh, blood and bone.

(RAVANA screams like a wild beast. He turns on all fours – clawing at his face. He is unable to bear the pain of being in his own body. RAMA stands like a stone. RAVANA's screams bellow through the city of Lanka)

RAMA: Janaki. Janaki….

RAVANA: *(Pleading)* Do it. Please. I beg you. End me.

(RAMA plunges the weapon into the Rakshasa's heart. All turn to MANDODARI who is standing as though already absent, lost in the void of her own terrible design)

MANDODARI: *(To all of us who witness her, but really to herself)* Do you know what it is to be born woman into this realm? To be used and shaped before your soul or body are formed. To be had and discarded? Torn and broken. Waiting, waiting for reasons to make themselves plain. Until you understand there is no reason. Just plans we can grow in the dark. And wait for the day to take back what was stolen from us as girls.

LAKSHMANA: And so you sacrificed your own daughter?

MANDODARI: I thought she was safe because of the curse: If he ravaged a woman – he would die.

RAMA: *(In a whisper)* Did he touch her?

MANDODARI: *(Weeping)* I did not count on Ravana being willing to lose everything for a woman To give his life.

RAMA: DID HE TOUCH HER?

MANDODARI: When I saw the devotion he was capable of for a woman, after all…I left him to the fate he fashioned for himself.

RAMA: *(Weeping)* Sita?

MANDODARI: *(Weeping too)* I lost my way…Called her name. But once entered – there was no way back. *(She is silent)*
Take my life. It is yours.

RAMA: *(Shaking his head – broken)* Take it yourself. From me you will get nothing more.

MANDODARI: *(She turns from him to walk away)* We find it easy to pin the darkness of the world's story on a woman's breast. But I was made in Ravana's heart. Fired in his kiln. The product of his male soul. While they fight out their ownership of us on battlefields, can they ever know the suffering we must endure? We become what shapes us. We learn to survive alone.

(To RAMA) Tell Sita that I love her; loved her the day I laid her in the earth that morning; love her still. I chose the left hand way – for though I loved her…I hated her father more.

(She turns and walks out into the wilderness. RAMA is on his knees)

6. Home

I.

(HANUMAN is kneeling before SITA-BODY who stands. Her face is bruised, streaked with dirt and tears. Her eyes are calm but she trembles from the violence still. SITA watches her body gently from a distance)

SITA-BODY: *(In a whisper)* Hanuman, Lord of Devotion. *(He lays himself at her feet)*

HANUMAN: Gracious one, Ravana is dead,

    (SITA-BODY kneels and kisses the ground. When she tries to rise, she stumbles. HANUMAN moves to help)

SITA-BODY: I will do it alone.

    (Which she does, with great pain and dignity)

    Has my Rama come for me?

HANUMAN: He waits outside.

    (Her eyes fill with tears of joy)

SITA-BODY: Tell him I am here when he is ready.

HANUMAN: He asked that we first bring you this holy water for the women to bathe you in and these finest silks in which you are to be dressed.

SITA-BODY: *(She looks at him for a long moment)* I need no silk or waters, Hanuman.

HANUMAN: He said to tell you: He cannot bear to see you in your suffering. He wishes you the time to gather your Self, and return to him as you once were.

SITA-BODY: *(To herself, grappling)* As she once was…

    (She looks over her shoulder at SITA who stands watching her. SITA-BODY is quiet. HANUMAN hands the fabric and perfumes to the women. As they move towards SITA, she raises her hand)

    Tell Rama I will meet him as I am.

(He nods, understanding her courage. He bows deeply, and turns to go)

Hanuman…

(He turns back to her)

Your devotion. Your heart…They go with me always.

(HANUMAN raises his hands together in humility to his forehead in thanks)

HANUMAN: As long as you are remembered, Devi – I will walk this world.

(He bows deeply again and then leaves her)

SITA: *(To the women)* Take those fabrics and perfumes for new brides at their beginning. Tell my Rama I am ready to be seen. As I am.

(The women around her bow and leave her. Alone, she looks over her shoulder at SITA, who nods, smiles gently and with great love. She is ready to go out)

II.

(Outside, RAMA is anxious)

(LAKSHMANA, VIBHEESHANA, SUGRIVA and HANUMAN look at one another, unsure of RAMA's intention. They wait with unease. Finally SITA-BODY appears and walks towards RAMA. Despite her ravaged state, she is incandescent. RAMA's eyes fill with tears. All internal conflict falling away, he looks at her with profound love)

RAMA: *(Whispers)* My Love.

SITA-BODY: My Lord.

(They stand looking at one another in silence. The VALMIKIS sing softly of love. SITA BODY reaches to wipe RAMA's tears. But with titanic effort, he holds his hand up and turns his face away. SITA-BODY is stunned)

Rama?

RAMA: *(In a whisper)* Sita. But no longer mine. *(SITA-BODY exhales as though struck)*

SITA: *(Standing at a distance, watching)* This body…

RAMA: Once touched…can never be untouched again.

SITA: …Was made only for sorrow.

SITA-BODY: *(Gathering herself, she is trembling, but centred now)* My Lord.
Your Wife stands before you.
Honour her.
She has travelled a great distance over time.

RAMA: *(His face twisted with conflict)* What man takes home his
wife, fresh from Ravana of Lanka's bed?

SITA-BODY: What man speaks such words to me?

RAMA: Rama of Ayhoda speaks.

SITA-BODY: *(Shaking her head)* No. The ego shadow is a fine
sand that blows into the finest cracks. But not the heart of my
Rama. For there is no space in there – not occupied by love.

RAMA: Do you know who you are, Sita of Lanka?

SITA-BODY: *(Looking him directly in the eyes)* I, my Lord, am Sita of
Time.
Daughter to The Great Mother.
Reeling back in over circles of pain.

RAMA: It has been said…

SITA-BODY: *(Interrupting him firmly but gently)* I care nothing for
what is said. Only for what is.

RAMA: *(With despair)* Who are you?

SITA: In this life I am called Sita. Wife to you in all.

RAMA: Did he touch you? Your father…

SITA-BODY: *(Tenderly, with hand on her heart)* Only you touch me.

RAMA: *(Losing control)* DID HE TOUCH YOU?

SITA: *(Steadfast)* Only you.

RAMA: *(Unable to look at her or to look away)* Your body is now
his…

SITA-BODY: This body?
This body is not his to take.

Nor yours to have.
Or mine to give.
I have loaned it from the Great Mother. Like everything, she will soon take it back. But who I am – the flame that burns within this clay – is mine to offer. And that light has been yours since the day we first met at the river, both barely 16 summers grown.

(RAMA shakes his head, eyes closed, in deepest battle with himself. His voice trembles with emotion)

RAMA: The body is sacred…

SITA-BODY: Body, my love, is subject to the wind: The manifestation of all we have lived. There is that which we choose for it – and that which others will write on our skin. But in matters of the soul – our choices are always our own. And I chose You. Even as you show me your shadow now – I choose you again.

(She reaches for his hand, but he cannot respond. She speaks softly)

Come with me, beloved, back into the dark forest of our love.
Forward into the blinding light of tomorrow.
Come with me, to a place beyond this body I must wear.
Let's walk beside one another along the narrow, overgrown path –
Back, back to when we are no longer afraid.

(The VALMIKIS sing softly of love)

RAMA: *(RAMA turns from her)* I swore to rescue you.
I owe you nothing more.

SITA-BODY: You who has known me better than I know myself,
You who has touched the dark waters of my soul

RAMA: *(With resolve)* Build a fire. Walk the flames of truth and prove your purity for everyone here.

SITA-BODY: Am I not standing in the centre of your fire right now?
It is more intense than anything you could manifest from wood.
I burn with questions you would have no answers for.

Questions that would make Ash of your small, frightened words.

But here is my love evident: I do not turn away.
I see your fear and I sing to you across the shifting, barren desert sands:
Beloved, do not be afraid.
Come with me, where nothing binds us to the womb of this small world.
Come with me to the edge of the forest to slip away in the dark.
Let's chase the lengthening shadows to the end of Danaka Vana and lie in her arms.

(RAMA covers his face. SITA looks on with great love. He looks up – gentle and broken now)

RAMA: Janaki, Janaki… My duty – before being a husband – is to be King. We cannot choose our Dharma. My people must come first. And they will always question your purity. How can I lead them when they doubt the very foundations of my own home?

SITA-BODY: Dance them through this shadow, Rama. They are frightened children who need you to light the way. Their fear for a woman's chastity is merely an infant's longing to have the Great Mother all to one's self. My "purity" lost is death your people fear. Yoni – the sacred Feminine Passage – brought us each life. But it threatens with proximity to the darkness from which we each barely emerged. Help your people to remember what it is, to love beyond ideas.

RAMA: Did he have you Janaki? I must know.
Did you surrender to Ravana's power?

SITA-BODY: Let only women speak of "surrender" for now. We bear children in the grip of death; we are humbled monthly by pain. Many of us have been forced flat and destroyed by another's violence – torn into against what we choose. Those who have endured this – know that it is possible to die… though the body lives on. To accuse us of "surrender" having survived this violation, is to fail us at love's most sacred core.

And when we are doubted by the very He whose name was the single mantra we uttered again and again just to survive… This a pain more profound than the profanation of one's own womb. Stand beside me and let me find that not my body – but the Turning Divinity in me – is my true worth in your eyes.

(RAMA is weeping softly)

(She whispers) Come with me, my love, back to where the forest grew around us like arms in love's dark, strong embrace. Come with me to where the light of tomorrow shines and life flourishes despite the fear and the pain.

(RAMA covers his face)

RAMA: Forgive me, my love. Forgive me. I am only a man.

SITA-BODY: In this messy struggle with the soul – not your godly perfection, but simply Rama the Man – can talk to us from the pain of being mortal and small. It is the imperfect Rama who will finally lead us home.

RAMA: *(Gathering her towards him)* He hurt you, my love…

SITA-BODY: Yes. But I am here.
And if I am Ravana's daughter… In the darkness of his longing – he ravaged only himself. Weep for Ravana of Lanka. He is all of us in the vortex of hunger. He is innocence who forgot that, in this life – we all answer to the same family name.

RAMA: *(Kneeling before her)* Keeper of the Dharma. Mother to us all.

(She takes his face in her hands and looks into his eyes)

SITA-BODY: Rama, take me home.

(KUSA and LAVA sing out as RAMA and SITA dissolve into dark)

178

III.

(The shape of their bodies form again in white light, moving as though on horseback, through the lands they left. RAMA sits behind SITA-BODY, holding her close as KUSA and LAVA sing. LAKSHMANA, VIBHEESHANA, HANUMAN, SUGRIVA ride nearby. SITA watches them go)

VALMIKI 1: Ayhoda, like Lanka, has nine city gates. Nine entry points to the heart. And we can only know the joy of coming home for the painful blessing of having left at all.

RAMA: *(Standing where he once stood to say goodbye to his birth-land)* Land of my ancestors, Gods of Kosala: Thanks be for this day of our return.

(He kisses the Earth. SITA-BODY does the same behind him – as does the rest of the traveling party. KAUSALYA, whose hair is now entirely white, walks towards and embraces them. She is frail, but as present as ever)

SITA: What lands we had wandered to in the shadows of our souls. The ocean's salt tide in us, pulled back to Ayhoda. At last the time of Ramaraja was here. You gave Ayhoda the heartbeat it had longed for. Some say those days lasted eleven thousand years. Never had any leader the devotion of the people like you, beloved.

(SITA watches from the shadows as RAMA lies over the SITA-BODY)

KAUSALYA: Yoni-Lingam – the sacred union: Perfect in the struggle and imperfection. Lingam pushes forward into the dark archway. And into life it is borne. The going into is where we find entry to the fires of this world.

SITA: And the night came to pass when I dreamed of twin boys singing to me from my womb.

(RAMA lies beside SITA-BODY and runs his hand over her large pregnant belly)

Our sons had emerged from the dense static of the In –
Between;
Into the gateway of that first single heart beat They were, at last, safely in my body of this world.

(The Street Boys continue their desolate, beautiful song)

IV.

(RAMA is seated in a circle, in counsel with KAUSALYA, LAKSHMANA and VIBHEESHANA. SITA-BODY remains in repose at the centre, asleep. Her huge belly is the manifest reason they are gathered. In reality, she lies in another room)

RAMA: Sita's time draws near.

KAUSALYA: We count the days that her tide brings your sons, as we *(smiling)* of failing eyes and yellowed teeth – prepare to slip back into the waters that once brought us to these shores.

RAMA: *(He nods to his mother and looks around at the trusted faces)*
My sacred circle who guard and protect me – heart, body, soul…
I have heard whisperings and want to know if what I fear is true: Tell me what my people say of Sita and the new lives she carries now.

(There is a deep silence of sudden unease. SITA-BODY sighs quietly and repositions her sleeping form. RAMA looks at his consorts – waiting, yet knowing that he will hear what he fears most)

Vibheeshana? Brother of Lanka once – but now to us all:
What is it my subjects whisper when they see my Sita pass, heavy with salt waters and new life?

(VIBHEESHANA is silent, looking at his hands, trembling with emotion as RAMA watches him and waits)

VIBHEESHANA: *(Quietly)* They speak of how Rama is just and fair and true. They pray every morning and evening that the reign of Rama never end for us all.

RAMA: *(After a long pause)* Lakshmana? Brother to my blood…

LAKSHMANA: *(He, too, is struggling)* They speak of your impeccable Dharma; How you made your bow sing across the battlefield before you felled Ravana of Darkness; How in courage – you have no equal. Never will.

(RAMA is silent. Finally he turns to KAUSALYA)

RAMA: Mother – perhaps only a woman will have the courage to tell me what my people say?

(KAUSALYA and all the women – SITA-BODY, SITA, VALMIKIS – all deeply inhale)

KAUSALYA: *(She turns and looks RAMA deep in the eyes. And though hers fill with tears, she never looks away)* They say that your Sita is a stain on the Ishvaku name.

(The room is thick with silence. KAUSALYA continues. She speaks now without pause)
They say that which is touched can never be untouched again. They say that if their King accepts a woman who has known the weight of another man, then what is to stop their wives from laying down where they may grow dark with flies. They say the twin boys Sita carries are the children of Ravana of Lanka. Others whisper that the unborn boys lie in her womb, hand in hand: One... the son of Rama Blue Prince of Grace. The other... the spawn of the Rakshasa's loins. And that we will never know which babe comes in darkness, until it's too late. They whisper that for you they would walk the earth over jagged glass – but that Sita should be taken with her unborn sons, so deep into Danaka Vana – that she never find her way to Ayhoda again. She is loved fiercely by the People. They need her. They weep to see her. They kiss her hands and take the dust from her feet. They know the depth of what she is. But they wait, like wolves when the scent is on the wind, to see her destroyed.

(KAUSALYA and all the women – SITA-BODY, SITA, VALMIKIS – all exhale deeply)

That, my son, is the truth I offer from my bones.

RAMA: *(Looking directly at KAUSALYA)* Thank you, ma.

(RAMA rises and walks away to stand alone. He covers his head and face with his hands. He speaks softly with himself – the despair and grief soaking through the whispered words. He is praying for strength. The others wait in respectful silence where he has left them. All of them keep their eyes cast down. SITA walks to RAMA gently and kisses his forehead – though he cannot see her. SITA-BODY murmurs in her sleep. The VALMIKIS begin a low note of chanting. RAMA gathers himself and returns to where the others wait)

(With numbed detachment)

Sita wishes to visit a great rishi's asrama for his blessing
tomorrow and plans to spend the night. In the morning,
Lakshmana, you will cross the Ganga and ride beyond the
frontiers of Kosala. You will bring Sita to the banks of Tamasa
– as she expects. But *(almost breathless)* she will never return
to Ayhoda in this lifetime again. You will leave her and her
unborn sons alone there.

*(LAKSHMANA and VIBHEESHANA gasp. KAUSALYA is silent,
breathlessly watching her son)*

LAKSHMANA: This! Because the people talk?

RAMA: I am here to serve. Without the people's faith, I cannot
lead. Though they love her, they doubt her purity still…

*(They are silent. LAKSHMANA looks up at RAMA finally – with steel
in his eyes)*

LAKSHMANA: Abandon Sita on the shores of the wild, pregnant
and alone?

This, Rama, you will have to do for yourself!

*(RAMA looks at LAKSHMANA. They stare deeply at one another. It is
a look of bitter challenge from LAKSHMANA that has never been there
before)*

VIBHEESHANA: *(Gently, trying reason)* Lord Rama, the people
will never understand a chastity like Sita's. Teach them. They
long for you to show the way.

RAMA: *(Without having taken his eyes from LAKSHMANA's, he speaks
with grim resolve)* Brothers, you will do as I have said, or you
may no longer call Ayhoda home.

(With emotion straining to break through)

Tell her I was called away urgently.
I cannot say goodbye. My strength will fail me.
Now go!

*(LAKSHMANA backs out of the room, longing for RAMA to change
what he has ordered him to do. They all leave – except KAUSALYA who*

remains. She walks around him to face him. He looks at her – his face now contorted with conflict and pain. She takes his face in her hands and stares deeply into his eyes)

KAUSALYA: Do you know who you are, son?

RAMA: Who am I, mother? Who am I? King. But only a man. Yet I am called to sacrifice what I value most.

(RAMA falls to his knees, praying for strength. KAUSALYA holds his head against her belly as he weeps like a child. All the women begin to hum)

KAUSALYA: Will there ever come a time when we understand just how much fear, how much hatred is inspired by our form. From us they emerge. Into us – they penetrate. At us they hurl their stones and hate. And in us curl like a child when once again alone. Shadow lives like its own pregnancy – ever waiting to have us borne back into the dark eye of the storm.

(She holds him a moment longer and then walks away, leaving him broken and sobbing on his knees on the floor)

V.

(LAKSHMANA rows, watching SITA-BODY, who is facing the water at the small boat's helm. She is radiant with joy. When they are midstream, SITA-BODY folds her hands and prays to the Ganga. When she is finished, she looks out onto the waters with a hand on her belly)

SITA-BODY: Ganga – whom the Devis bathed in...

(She looks behind her when she hears LAKSHMANA's trembling breath)

Lakshmana?

LAKSHMANA: I was just remembering when we last crossed her...

SITA-BODY: But this time we know we will return home.

(When they reach land, LAKSHMANA, despite himself, buckles over with the pain)

SITA-BODY: Brother, what is it?

(She watches him for a moment and then her spine straightens)

(She nods, turns and walks away. He goes after her. He catches her as she falls)

SITA-BODY: *(Crying out with her whole soul)* This body was made only for sorrow.

(LAKSHMANA can only weep. Slowly she gathers herself and pulls away)

Tell them not to grieve for me, brother. For I am now gone.
I will never return in this life again.
Go now while you have strength.

(He walks around her in pradakshina, weeping silently. He lays at her feet and she blesses him)

Dear Lakshmana…You who has watched over me always:
May you forgive yourself and find peace again someday.

(He stands and looks her in the eyes. Then he turns and steps into the boat. She watches as it leaves the shore, and then the shadows fall around and over her as she disappears into the dark)

(A shadow of the great eagle JATAVU moves overhead. The plastic covers on the scaffolding tremor and KUSA and LAVA begin to sing)

VI.

(SITA-BODY lies dead, face down – arms stretched wide in the earth's embrace. KAUSALYA and MANDODARI as VALMIKI SAMAJ stand beside the corpse)

VALMIKI 1: No one knows how she survived alone on those shores. She held on until her due time came to push her twin boys into the world.

(LAKSHMANA's boat is passing through the dark water. His face is buried in his hands. He looks up)

LAKSHMANA: Who's there?

(A boat like his own moves through the waters in the direction from where he came. He stares through the mist and dark, trying to make out who stands, watching the water beneath their boat)

Who passes these waters in silence when a friend calls out?

(LAKSHMANA raises his bow and takes aim)

Answer me or I must take you as my enemy. Speak now.

(The figure answers back quietly. It is the voice of RAMA – though the person shadowed)

RAMA-FIGURE: When we watched the rain fall as small boys
in our secret cave, I used to weep. And you sat beside me
in silence and faith with a piece of bread, ready to serve me
when my hunger woke. Brother – do not look for Rama. He is
now gone. His Dharma was to serve his people. And the only
way to lead is to show them what they have lost.

SITA: *(Smiling at RAMA gently and reaching over SITA-BODY and the
waters)* Come with me, beloved, back into the dark forest of
our love.
Forward into the blinding light of tomorrow's promise.
Come. Let us run through time.
Like children, when once we were not afraid.

VALMIKI 2: *(Standing with the other sanitation women around the
SITA-BODY)* We found her in death – just as Janaka had found
her at dawn in a furrow of the earth, when she herself was
borne. Lying in the dark arms of her Mother – at last she had
been gathered her home.

*(VIBHEESHANA is at RAMA's side, trying to wake him. He is naked,
lying in a fetal position)*

VIBHEESHANA: My Lord? My Lord? Wake up. The light has
long come and gone.

*(He listens at his chest and then sits up – a cry of mourning erupting
from him)*

RAMA-FIGURE: *(To LAKSHMANA who continues to listen on the dark
waters)*
Until the queen, the base, the great holder of the sacred
passage and heart, keeper of the Dharma, mother to us all…is
welcome – Rama-Sita cannot call this Home.

SITA: *(Stretching out her arms from the shore over the dead SITA-BODY)*
Come with me, my Love, where nothing binds us to the
womb of this small world.

Come with me to the edge of the forest's warm nights…to slip away and be wild hearts again, in the fires of everything we hold.

(KAUSALYA is at VIBHEESHANA's side now, looking at the empty body of RAMA, lying curled up on the floor. She loosens her long white hair, removes her shoes and sits on the floor beside her son. She pulls his dead body into her embrace)

KAUSALYA: *(As though she now understands)* Only a man, my son.
But True King after all.
You were leaving us – never her.
I understand now why you wept, my only boy.

VALMIKI 2: Lying in the arms of the Mother – the flies already breaking down what we believe is forever ours. But always She will have the final word.

(The women are gathered around the SITA-BODY. They turn her over and find two newborn boys. The women lift the babies)

At her breasts…Lava and Kusa – a few hours. Old.

(They move slowly away to her left and right. The umbilical chords remain attached getting longer and longer, with the SITA-BODY still connected to them: A ragged goddess wired to these two new babies. The STREET BOYS sing their wild and urgent song of the vedas, calling us on the street. Urban rhythms grow with the sound)

We took them in and taught them the song of their birthright – to be sung as long as there are men and women in the world.

LAKSHMANA: *(To the figure in the shadows of the boat beside his)* But who will lead us if you are gone?

RAMA-FIGURE: My rightful heirs.

VALMIKI 2: On every corner we pass – they call to us still.

RAMA – FIGURE: There is no Ayhoda but the heart of the people. On the street, they will carry the word…

VALMIKI 1: Our unclaimed children who travel the ages, to call us up from our slumber; To cast off numbness; To remember all we have lost.

LAKSHMANA: Who speaks to me, if Rama is gone?

RAMA-FIGURE: I came – as Matsya, Kurma, Varaha, Narasimha, Vamana and Parasurama – every age to manifest dharma. Incarnated as a kshatriya this time, but always, Lord Vishnu himself: Come again from age to age to protect and repair our world. He who brings this message is Yama Deva – Death himself.

(SITA opens her arms as RAMA's boat reaches her shores. They fold into each other's powerful embrace)

KAUSALYA: It is she who holds him at the base of his power. The surrendering that tears down all arguments against the thrusting sea. The capacity to hold and hold him – while he battles the coming storms.

VALMIKI 1: But who among us will recognize ourselves, when finally, all the mathematics of time contrive to have us pass by the very street corner, just as our story is sung? To fall to our knees in recognition. To grieve and finally die into life.

(KUSA and LAVA sing full voiced as the WOMEN lift the SITA-BODY. They make supplications to the SITA-BODY organs – asking them to return to their sources. They are chanting)

Vision returns to the Sun.
Mind to the Moon
Body to the ground.
And Prana – Breath of Life – to the cosmic eternal that is without end.

(The SITA-BODY exhales a thin stream of mist. The plastic sheets covering the scaffolding and walls are released and float to the ground)

(The vedic chants assume an increasing contemporary urban rythm – as the stage fills with the company dressed in modern urban gear – all attached to ipods, chords and one another – passing around KUSA and LAVA singing – who stand in downtown urban chaos, plastic bags swirling around their feet)

Epilogue

(SITA and RAMA watch from the periphery, hand in hand)

SITA: Do not grieve for us, beloveds. For we are now gone. Freer
than you are, still in the body of pain.
Made only for sorrow.
But from sorrow we have much to learn.
Burn after reading it – but read it well.
The beauty, the loss, the grieving.
There on the skin, in those bones, beneath those feet you have
worn for this life.
On every street corner – Ayhoda calls.

(Turning into the darkness with RAMA, she looks back one last time)

We wait in the moving Danaka Vana.
Look for us.
We are there.

(SITA-RAMA slips away into black)

*(The Vedas, sung by the STREET BOYS fill the space, throbbing with
urgency, as lights fade. Only the cyclorama glows – filled with a static
snow pattern once again.*

*HANUMAN – in a single shaft of light – reaches out to catch something
soft that floats down into his open palm. Blackout)*

ENDS

MIES JULIE

My gratitude to:

Lara Foot

The cast who originated these roles.

The entire team at The Baxter Theatre Centre, Cape Town.

Jonathan Garfinkel; Tanya Farber and Aubrey Sechabe.

The Farber-Daniel family for their support during the
creation period

and

Ella Altidor – for bearing the upheavals in your
little world.

Mies Julie was commissioned and originally produced by the Baxter Theatre Centre at the University of Cape Town, and premiered at the National Arts Festival, Grahamstown, South Africa, on July 8, 2012 with the following cast:

Mies Julie	Hilda Cronje
John	Bongile Mantsai
Christine	Thoko Ntshinga
Ukhokho	Tandiwe Nofirst Lungisa

Director	Yaël Farber
Music composed & performed by	Matthew & Daniel Pencer
Singer & musician	Tandiwe Nofirst Lungisa
Set design	Patrick Curtis
Costume design	Birrie le Roux
Lighting design	Paul Abrams
Sound design	Philip Botes

Mies Julie premiered in the United Kingdom at the Assembly Hall in Edinburgh on August 9, 2012.

Mies Julie premiered in North America at St. Ann's Warehouse, Brooklyn, NY, on November 8, 2012.

Mies Julie	Hilda Cronje
John	Bongile Mantsai
Christine	Thoko Ntshinga
Ukhokho	Tandiwe Nofirst Lungisa

Director	Yaël Farber
Music composed & performed by	Matthew & Daniel Pencer
Singer & musician	Tandiwe Nofirst Lungisa
Set design	Patrick Curtis
Costume design	Birrie le Roux
Lighting design	Patrick Curtis
Sound design	Philip Botes

'Awaking on Friday morning, June 20, 1913,
the South African Native found himself, not actually a slave,
but a pariah in the land of his birth.'

Sol Plaatje

Characters

MIES JULIE
Afrikaans daughter of a farmer, early 20s

JOHN
Xhosa man, a servant on the farm, late 20s

CHRISTINE
Xhosa woman, mother to John, a domestic
worker on the farm who raised Julie, mid-60s

UKHOKHO
Xhosa woman, other-wordly ancestor of
indeterminate age

SETTING
A farmhouse kitchen.
Eastern Cape – Karoo, South Africa.
Freedom Day 2012

MISE EN SCENE

The kitchen is defined simply by an oxblood-coloured floor, which sits like an island in the centre of the endless planes of the Karoo's bleak beauty. Downstage right, the floor's stone tiles are ruptured by a truncated tree stump and its surrounding roots – which protrude and have spread along the floor. There is: a kitchen table and chairs; a stove on which a pot smoulders with steam; a small bench that John sits on to polish boots; a larger bench lined with rubber gumboots and rough farming implements (sickle, panga/machete, pitchfork, spade, sheering scissors). A birdcage hangs upstage right, just outside of the defined kitchen area. Its shape should resemble a small house. A large pair of lace-up leather boots stands alone. Their power is obvious.

A fan circles slowly, listlessly overhead.

UKHOKHO is always present on the periphery, watching. At times she enters the kitchen space when indicated. At other times, she returns to her observer stance – a discreet presence on the periphery.

1.

Night. The heat is stifling.

CHRISTINE is on all fours, scrubbing the stone floor. She is sweating profusely. She sings a circular phrase – a soft atonal moan from a church spiritual. She periodically scrapes an enamel bucket along the floor so that it remains by her side as she cleans. JULIE enters and walks circles – aching with boredom and loneliness. She sits at the table, her feet up. She rises and walks across the floor – leaving footprints. CHRISTINE follows behind and erases them without a change of expression. JULIE disappears into the night. JOHN stands at the door, watching his mother, who continues her work unawares. He has a large 'throw' about his neck and shoulders.

JOHN: *(Watching where she left.)* She's mad again tonight, ma. Bewitched.

Looking out across the night sky.

It's a dark night. Where's this moon? Supposed to be full.

CHRISTINE: The swallows are flying low. We'll have rain after midnight – when this heat breaks.

JOHN: *(To himself.)* Ja[1]... Dangerous. Coming to our party like that.

CHRISTINE: Poor baby. She's been wild since Baas[2] Jan broke off the engagement.

CHRISTINE goes to the stove and brings JOHN a plate of food. They bow their heads and pray.

---

1   **Yes** *(Afrikaans)*
2   **boss** *(Afrikaans; a term not always specific to an employer but indicates subservience on the speaker's part.)*

JOHN: Salt?

CHRISTINE: Hayi kaloku![3] Taste first.

He tastes and indicates for the salt. She hands it to him with playful annoyance. He adds generously. She snatches it away. He moves to his bench, and sits. He eats.

Indicating a chair at the kitchen table.

You can sit to eat. Meneer[4] is away.

He glances about – then moves to the table, sits and eats.

CHRISTINE is peeling potatoes now.

JOHN: *(Looking towards the stove.)* What's that stink?

CHRISTINE: It's for Julie's dog, Diana.

JOHN: You have to cook for her dog now too?

CHRISTINE: She's pregnant. Miesie[5] wants me to take care of it. The bitch was in heat last month and all the pedigree dogs from around here wanted her.

JOHN: I heard them howling. I thought it was just the moon.

CHRISTINE: But our Swartkop got her. Klein Mies[6] was furious. She says the dog betrayed her. *(Stirring the foul fluid.)* She asked me to prepare something that will kill the puppies in the womb.

---

3   **Taste first!** *(isiXhosa)*
4   **Mister** *(Afrikaans; a title indicating subservience towards the subject on the part of the speaker.)*
5   **miss** *(Afrikaans; a term of respect that indicates subservience on the speaker's part.)*
6   **little miss** *(Afrikaans; a term of address used by black South African employees when referring to the children of their white employers.)*

JOHN: *(To himself.)* Mies Julie… She's dancing wild out there with our boys – but she won't let her bitch touch ours. She's like all white women. Too proud. But not proud enough. Maybe she'll blow her brains out – like her mama.

CHRISTINE: Haai![7] I don't want such talk in my kitchen. I want you to go get her and bring her back here.

JOHN: I'm still eating, ma.

CHRISTINE folds her arms and stares at her son.

The new boys were asking how come you can you cook for me in here – and they're out there with no electricity or water.

CHRISTINE: This is *my* kitchen. They will never understand how things work around here. They come to Veenen Plaas[8] and want to take what we've been working for all our lives.

JOHN: When winter comes – our children will freeze. Meneer refuses to turn the heat and water back on until we chase the squatters away. It's a brutal way. Punishing *us* to get them off the land.

CHRISTINE: They must build their shacks somewhere else. Meneer doesn't want them living here.

JOHN: He's a hard boer[9]. By law they have the right to live here – if their parents did. A storm is coming to this farm. The workers are celebrating Freedom tonight, but there is anger on the wind out there.

---

7   **Hey!** *(vernacular)*
8   **The Weeping Farm** *(Old Dutch; the name of the farm)*
9   **farmer** *(Afrikaans)*

199

CHRISTINE: This is Meneer's land. He decides. Finished and klaar[10].

JULIE enters the kitchen. JOHN stands immediately – caught in the forbidden act of sitting at the family table. But JULIE paces, preoccupied. JOHN finishes eating on his feet, and then goes to his bench to polish the Meneer's boots. CHRISTINE stirs the concoction at the stove. Mother and son surreptitiously watch JULIE , who is unaware of their gaze.

CHRISTINE: Rain coming tonight Miesie. I can smell it.
The ants are moving faster. The clouds gathering low.

JULIE doesn't respond. She lies back, full length, on the kitchen table.

I'll go give this to Diana.
It won't be easy on her. The pregnancy's too far already.

But I'll do my best.

She strokes JULIE's hair and then goes out, looking for the dog.

JOHN removes the 'throw' from his shoulders and drops it to the floor. He begins polishing the Meneer's boots. Nothing for sometime but JULIE – who rises and paces – and John working at the boots. JULIE is restless, preoccupied, wanting. JOHN watches her when she cannot see him.

When she can, he is inscrutable in servitude.

JULIE: I was looking for you.

JOHN: *(Stands.)* Do you need me, mies?

JULIE: Come back to the party and dance.

---

10 **finished** *(Afrikaans; 'finished and klaar' is a South African expression, connoting 'end of discussion')*

JOHN: Don't go back there looking for trouble, mies.

JULIE: Niemand sal aan my raak nie.[11] My pa will shoot the black man in the head that puts his hands on me. Then he'll shoot me. Told me that once when I was little. That was my bedtime story. *(She laughs.)*

Come. Dance with me.

JOHN: You drunk, Mies Julie. Go to bed.

JULIE: Scared?
Don't worry. My father wouldn't touch you. You're his favourite. Likes you more than he ever liked me. Always wanted a boy.

She looks away, out into the night.

It's dry out there. Bleached yellow white. This time of year always reminds me when I was a kid. You know. After my ma. The open veldt[12] fires. She used to come home from her midnight walks – her hair smelling like wood smoke and burnt leaves. Smells like my ma out there.

He continues his work in silence.

What's your problem? It's just dancing.

JOHN: Don't try be one of us tonight, Mies. They're celebrating with anger out there. I can't protect you like before. Just go to bed.

JULIE: We cannot have the squatters build their shacks on our land…

---

11   **No one will touch me.** *(Afrikaans)*
12   **field** *(Afrikaans)*

But I don't agree with how my father is doing it. I'm not like him, you know.

He does not respond.

Christine will never forgive you – if something happens to me out there. Your mama will punish you if I get hurt. Just like she used to when we were small.

She backs out the door, daring him. JOHN sits alone for a while, cleaning the boots. He stops and stares ahead. He is filled with anger and desire for her. Kwaito music[13] drifts in and out on the wind. He stands and paces the kitchen. He suddenly dances alone. He walks out into the night, towards the music.

The kitchen stands empty. A low electronic hum begins, as UKHOKHO rises from where she has been watching. Softly playing her harmonica, she walks the periphery of the kitchen. CHRISTINE, humming to herself, returns with the empty dog plate. She moves into the kitchen and immediately senses the presence of her ancestor. She drops the plate with a clatter. She is frozen – staring trance-like.

JOHN enters and moves swiftly to his mother.

JOHN: Ma, you alright?

CHRISTINE: Ndiyamva.[14] She is here again, son.

JOHN: Who, ma?

CHRISTINE: When she's restless, I can smell her.

I can smell the damp.

JOHN is silent with grave concern, watching his mother.

---

13 *A variant of house music that emerged in Johannesburg, South Africa in the 1990s. It remains most popular amongst the black youth of South Africa.*

14 **She is here again, son** *(isiXhosa)*

I've told her: Ndimxelele Ukhokho![15] You must rest now. Eat soil and be quiet. Meneer will throw me off Veenen Plaas if I break the floor again. Don't disturb my head. She just laughs and shows me where the roots of the tree are cracking through these stones.

JOHN: Did you faint again, ma?

On her knees, her hands running over the tree's roots.

CHRISTINE: I used to play in this tree when I was a girl. Before this farmhouse was built. When there was nothing here but open veldt.

JOHN: That wasn't you ma. That was your grandmother. Remember? When you were born – this house was already here.

CHRISTINE: Kuthe Thabalala.[16] And this tree belonged only to the wind.

JOHN: Ma –

On her knees, patting the kitchen floor.

CHRISTINE: Our ancestors are all buried in this field. But when the Meyers built this house, they cut the tree down and laid a kitchen over the graves.

JOHN: Don't talk about this in front of Meneer, ma.

CHRISTINE: After the madam died, they tore up the kitchen floor. The roots were still alive in the concrete. Fat and wet and full of the earth's blood under those old tiles.

---

15 **Rest, ancestor!** *(isiXhosa)*
16 **Just open land.** *(isiXhosa)*

JOHN: Ma, sukuthetha ngezizinto.[17]

CHRISTINE: That tree was here before any of us. We planted it over your great grandmother's grave. And under the roots, lies Ukhokho. This tree saps from her bones. Your great grandmother won't let me sleep until I free them from beneath.

She grabs a large garden fork nearby and attempts to attack the stones with the fork.

JOHN wrestles the implement from her hands.

JOHN: Don't break the floor again, mama!
I'm still paying for damages.

CHRISTINE: They can cover what they've done but the roots keep breaking through. These roots will never go away. Never. Never. Go away.

She is weeping. JOHN helps her to the bench. UKHOKHO slowly withdraws.

CHRISTINE cannot tear her eyes from the apparition. JOHN brings her water, which she gulps.

JULIE drifts in and sits, feet up on the table.

She has put an open bottle of wine on the table and has a glass in her hand.

CHRISTINE: *(Noticing JULIE, she attempts to hide her distress.)* You OK Miesie?

JULIE: I was dumped, Christine. The engagement is off. Everyone knows.

---

17 **Ma, better not talk of such things.** *(isiXhosa)*

Marrying him was my father's idea anyway. He needs a man to take over this place. I don't…need a man.

Did you give Diana the muti[18]?

CHRISTINE: Yes mies. I'll check on her now.

CHRISTINE stands.

JOHN: It's OK, ma. I'll do it.

JOHN helps his exhausted mother to a chair in the corner. CHRISTINE sits heavily. JOHN helps her settle. She closes her eyes. JULIE watches them suspiciously.

JULIE: What's wrong with her?

JOHN: She's just tired, Mies.

JULIE: I asked you to change.

JOHN: What does my madam want me to wear?

JULIE: Whatever you wear when you're not the Help. Be a man tonight, John. Not a 'boy'.

JOHN is sharpening a sickle. JULIE has her back to him. He watches her.

She senses his gaze and turns.

What are you staring at?

JOHN: *(Caught.)* Just remembering…

JULIE: What?

JOHN: You as a child.

18 medicine *(vernacular)*

JULIE: What do you remember?

JOHN: Things.

JULIE: Tell me.

JOHN: *(Glancing over at CHRISTINE.)* My mother's trying to sleep, mies.

JULIE: Then she should go to her room.

CHRISTINE has fallen asleep in her chair.

Come. Sit.

JOHN: Meneer doesn't like it.

JULIE: It's my table too – and I say: sit!

He doesn't move.

And if I order you?

JOHN: *(Shrugging.)* I'll do it.

JULIE: So sit.

Wary, he moves slowly to the table and sits.

Drink?

JOHN: I have to get up early.

JULIE: Don't make me drink alone, John.

She pours a glass of wine for him.

None of this 'Crackling'[19] poison you guys drink.
The best from my father's cellar.

(Cynically.) To Freedom.

He raises his glass.

Do you feel free?

JOHN: Sure.

JULIE: Good.
Now kiss my foot.

He rises and steps away from the table.

To show just how far we've come in almost twenty years!

He moves back to his bench.

(Viciously.) Fucking. Do. It.

Silently enraged, he stands and moves to her. He kneels and reaches for her foot. She slips it away from his grasp. In a flash, he grabs her foot and puts it on his shoulder. He runs his hand up her thigh towards her crotch. He runs his open mouth over the top of her foot. She is stunned. And aroused. He moves away.

JOHN: Get out of here, Mies Julie!

JULIE: *(Flustered.)* You afraid?

JOHN: Just go, please.

He is glancing at the windows.

---

19 *An extremely cheap, poor quality wine that farm labourers commonly drink in South Africa's farmlands.*

JULIE: *(Realizing.)* You worried what the other workers will say…

JOHN: Everyone was already talking, mies.

JULIE: Why do you care?

JOHN: I live with them.

JULIE: I live with them too.

JOHN: No you don't. You live in this house. I live out there.

JULIE: Am I supposed to feel sorry for you?

JOHN: You not supposed to feel anything for me, mies.
     You don't know how much bitterness is out there.
     Let's just not be alone, ok?

JULIE: We're not. Your mother is here.

JOHN: Sleeping.

JULIE: Then I'll wake her.
     Christine. CHRISTINE.

CHRISTINE mumbles in her sleep.

(Roughly.) HEY WENA![20] CHRISTINE!

JOHN: Leave her alone, mies.
     She's been working since sunrise.

JULIE: I heard you talking about my ma.
     I remember the day she died. You…

---

20 **You!** *(isiXhosa)*

JOHN: What?

JULIE: Cried. I came out of the church and everyone was watching me – hungry eyes. You were the only one not looking. You had your hat in your hands. Your mouth was trembling. You cried for her.

JOHN: No. For you.

JULIE: *(They stare at each other.)*
Come with me.
I want to show you where I go some nights.

JOHN: No.

JULIE: I'll bring my dad's gun.

JOHN: It's not that. I can protect you.

JULIE: You don't want to be seen.

JOHN: They're stupid with anger, mies. They won't understand.

JULIE: I respect them more than you do.

JOHN: Times have changed. They don't care if you do.

JULIE: But they do. Respect me.

JOHN: No. They don't. They need you.
And your father. They need a job.
They eat your bread. But they laugh at you behind your back.

JULIE: That's cruel.

JOHN: And if I walk out there with you – they will laugh at me too. Now I have to walk with you, and laugh with them about you afterwards. I'm not going to do that.

JULIE: You're strong.

JOHN: Yes.

JULIE: Some nights I just want to walk into the Karoo[21]. Like the poet who walked into the sea.[22] Beneath the pylons like huge mothers, arms folded – watching me. Out into the veldt until I reach the Power Station. She used to go there at night. She liked to stand beside it. Listen to it sing. And in my dream I'm there. I start to dig. My fingers are bleeding. Suddenly the hard ground gives way and I am falling. And I want this. To be falling. Do you dream?

JOHN: Every night. I'm a boy again. Reaching into a black eagle's nest to steal eggs. But they keep slipping – covered with salt and stickiness. I manage to get my hand around one. It's still warm. I don't realize it's a black mamba's nest I have my hand in. I feel the bite like a stab into the bone. I know I have minutes before I fall into the black sleep. I always wake up drowning – without air.

JULIE: Come with me. We can go out the back. No one will see us.

He suddenly holds his hand over his eye.

What is it?

JOHN: Mosquito in my eye.

JULIE: Laat ek sien.[23]

---

21 *A large elevated, semi-desert plateau in South Africa.*
22 *Reference to* **Ingrid Jonker** *(1933 – 1965) an iconic Afrikaans poet who committed suicide by walking into the sea.*
23 **Let me see** *(Afrikaans)*

JOHN: I'm ok.

JULIE: Let me see!

She leads him to sit and steps between his legs to look into his eye. She blows gently into the eye.

CHRISTINE wakes and yawns.

CHRISTINE: Kuqhubeka ntoni?[24]

JULIE: Mosquito in his eye, Christine.

CHRISTINE: Yithi ndibone.[25]

JOHN: Ndiright ma.[26]

CHRISTINE: Let me see.

JOHN: It's ok ma. Go to bed.

CHRISTINE: I have to check on Diana.
The storm is almost here. Even though we've repaired it – the roof is still leaking. Don't forget to put buckets out.

JOHN: Ndizakuzenza ngoku.[27]

CHRISTINE sings softly as she leaves. JULIE steps back between JOHN's legs.

JULIE: I almost had it…

JOHN: You're playing with fire, Mies Julie.

JULIE: Good thing I'm insured.

24 **What is it?** *(isiXhosa)*
25 **Come here** *(isiXhosa)*
26 **I'm ok mama** *(isiXhosa)*
27 **I'll do it now.** *(isiXhosa)*

JOHN: Ja. But I'm not.

He moves to go. She steps in his path, her body against his.

Don't test me, Mies Julie. I'm only a man.

He moves to kiss her mouth. She slaps him brutally across the face. He is stunned. He turns away in rage.

JULIE: Ah come on now. Don't sulk.

He picks up a boot and starts to polish it.

Put the boot down.

He ignores her, seething.

Put it down!
You're proud.

JOHN: No, I'm not! I'm just a groveling kaffir[28] boy – grateful for my job.

JULIE: *(Regretful.)* I'm sorry... Ek's jammer...[29]

He continues polishing.

(Close to tears.) I'm sorry.

They are both emotional and silent.

(After some time.) Have you ever loved a woman?
Have you? I mean like you couldn't eat. Couldn't sleep.

He looks at her.

---

28 *An offensive South African term for a black person.*
29 **I'm sorry...** *(Afrikaans)*

Who was she?

He looks away in shame. She realizes.

What?
Since when?

JOHN: Your mother came home from the hospital with you wrapped in a blanket. We were all waiting to welcome you. Your mother got out the car. Her face empty. No one behind her eyes. She put you in my mother's open hands and didn't look back once. Just walked into the shade of the dark house. My mother put you on the kitchen table. I stood on a chair to see. I remember the love on my mother's face when she first unwrapped that blanket.

She never looked at me like that.

Before you could walk – you were always in her arms or tied to her back.

JULIE: My ma was always on fire about something. Never about me.

JOHN: We love what our mothers love.

JULIE: And we hate what takes them away.

JOHN: When you were old enough to play with us – the kaffir kids – your father couldn't keep you away from me. Tried beating you. But nothing made you ashamed.

JULIE: School. Graaf Reniet taught me that.

JOHN: And your cousins – from Leeu-Gamka[30].

---

30 *A small town in the Western Cape Province of South Africa.*

JULIE: Hannes and Dirk?

JOHN: They would come every Christmas. They would always call me to play.

JULIE: *(Laughing.)* You were…

JOHN: The 'clever kaffir'. I know. One evening, Hannes is racing me to the swing tire in the willow tree.

JULIE: The rope is still there – rotten now though. It's become part of the tree.

JOHN: I was faster, stronger than Hannes that year. I can hear him swearing behind me. I reach the tire before him and jump in.

JULIE: I remember that year you won. The look on Hannes' face.

JOHN: I swing hard. High.
I know you are watching us from the stoep[31].
I feel something wet and warm on my back. I turn. Hannes has his dick out. He laughing with Dirk. Pissing on my back. I look up at the stoep. You are laughing too. You're beautiful. And cruel.
Then you are gone. Into the house.

JULIE: Childhood is brutal.

JOHN: Only for kaffir boys.

JULIE: No. For everyone.

JOHN: You don't know –

---

31 **veranda** *(Afrikaans)*

JULIE: I know.

JOHN: Later, I climb the tree by the farmhouse to see you.
I fall and land in the dog shit. The boere men come out
with dogs and guns. When they see it's just me – they start
laughing, kicking me. Your mama is watching from behind
the window. Dark eyes. My mama behind her. Nothing she
can do but watch. I run. I'm crying. I hide in the veldt. You
are out there. Playing alone.

JULIE: I always loved being out there. By that old windmill.

JOHN: You squat behind an aloe to pee. Your dress gets wet.
You take it off and hang it in a tree. Your breasts are just
starting. I lie there in the wet earth – stinking of dog shit –
watching you. Between being a woman and a child…

JULIE: I always felt you.

JOHN: A dog can be your pet. A horse your companion. But
a kaffir boy… What is he? I want to drown myself in the
dam but my uncle fishes me out and beats the shit out of
me. I go home. Mama washes me. We go to church.

JULIE: And then?

JOHN: I decide to die.

JULIE: How old were you?

JOHN: Maybe 14. If I can't have you – I want to disappear into
the harvest. Like I was never born. I wait for the night of
the full moon. I climb inside the silo and wait for morning
when they dump the new load. But my uncle follows me.
He lets the grain fall and bury me. Just as I stop breathing
– he pulls me out. To teach me a lesson. I vomited dust and
blood for weeks.

JULIE: Jussis.[32]

JOHN: Have you ever been loved like that?

JULIE: You loved me?
    Or you just hated yourself?

JOHN: Same thing.

They both smile.

JULIE: You different.

JOHN: I read.

JULIE: What do you read?

JOHN: Whatever I get my hands on. I'm not going to spend
    my life cleaning your father's boots.

JULIE: So what's the plan? It's a free country.

JOHN: I have a plan.

JULIE: Hoping for a hand out? Some land so that one by one,
    the farmlands return to black hands?

JOHN: Maybe.

JULIE: It's not some score to be settled, John. Farming is a business.
    And a tough one.

JOHN: Don't worry about me, mies.

JULIE: I worry about *me*. And my father. Here. The dogs were
    barking again last night. That low growling that wakes you
    up in the dark – breathless. Because you know someone

───────────────
32 **Jesus.** *(Afrikaans)*

who shouldn't be – is near. Some nights I go stand outside. I feel safer there. I sleep with my gun under my pillow.

JOHN: I know.
You need to get married, Mies Julie.

JULIE: What for? Someone comes in here to kill us – we both going to get a panga in the head. Why suffer marriage, if he can't even save me?

JOHN: Why did you push him away like that?

JULIE: He was afraid.

JOHN: Women always say that, when a man doesn't love them. Why can't they just say: He doesn't love me?

JULIE: Why can't men just say: I'm afraid?

JOHN: Of what?

JULIE: Everything. Mostly of women who love them. You're such cowards.

JOHN: I'm not afraid.

JULIE: How many women do you have?

JOHN: Enough.

JULIE: If you were not afraid – you wouldn't need more than one.

JOHN: I saw you in the stables with him.

JULIE: Spying on us.

JOHN: It was too late for me to leave. I saw you go down.
Your nose bleeding. On your knees. Crying. But strong.

They are so close, their bodies are touching.

JOHN: *(Pulling back.)* I'm going to bed.

JULIE: *(Catching his hand as he turns to go, she pushes him into a chair.)*
It's Freedom Day out there, John.

She lifts her skirt slowly. He watches. She straddles him.

He grasps her to him, overcome with desire. Suddenly, he pushes her off.

JOHN: This is just a game to you. But my mum and I – we
have nowhere else to go. She was born on this farm. Her
sweat is in these walls. Her blood – in this floor. Now I
must risk everything.
Because you're drunk and bored tonight.

JULIE: It's just a walk. I'm not asking you to marry me.

JOHN: I wouldn't – even if you asked!

She moves to strike him again. He grabs her wrists.

Slap me again – you better be ready.

JULIE: For what?

He shoves her at the table and tears her dress away.

JULIE: *(Vulnerable, panicked.)* What if the others come in?

JOHN: I'll kill anyone who comes through that door.

He pushes her flat onto her back on the kitchen table, tears away his overalls and penetrates her. She cries out. Realizing the gravity of what he is doing, he stumbles away from the table overwhelmed. He cannot stay away. He jumps onto the table. He lies on her and she embraces him. He fucks her hard. She weeps, overcome with emotion. He comes. They kiss passionately. Then tenderly. He whispers to her. JOHN falls asleep in JULIE's embrace. Light moves across the kitchen floor, as the hours pass. Thunder rumbles.

And while they are sleeping, CHRISTINE & UKHOKO rise from where they have been waiting on the periphery, and stand over the table, watching them. They sing in unearthly tones, with farming implemets over their shoulders. Is this JOHN's dream or a visitation? We will never know. They move across the room as they sing. CHRISTINE places tin buckets around the room to catch the water dripping through the roof. UKHOKHO lifts the Meneer's boots and places them centre stage. The women move away. CHRISTINE tips the birdcage as she leaves. It is still spinning like a small house in a storm as…

2.

JULIE wakes abruptly. It is still dark out, but morning will break soon. She sees JOHN sleeping beside her. She looks between her legs. There is blood on her thighs. Breathless with realization, her eyes scan the room. She gets off the table and walks the kitchen – looking at everything as though new. She sees her father's boots and buckles with fear and pain. She squats over a bucket and cleans her inner thighs. JOHN wakes and watches her.

JOHN: *(Gently.)* You OK?

> *She turns her naked body away and, finding JOHN's 'throw' nearby on the floor, she hangs it around her neck – covering her breasts.*

I was your first?

> *She nods. He pulls her into his embrace.*

You mine now.

JULIE: You love me? *(JOHN is silent but not unloving.)*

Say it.

JOHN: Not in this house. While those boots wait for me, mies.

JULIE: You call me 'mies'. After last night? *(She laughs softly through her tears.)*

JOHN: Habit.

JULIE: Break it.

JOHN: While we are still in this house – my skin, my hands belong to him.
Just looking at those boots makes my stomach hurt.

JULIE: You mine now. Not his.

JOHN: Not here.

JULIE: So let's leave.

JOHN: Now?

JULIE: I can't stay.

JOHN: I can't go.

JULIE: Why not?

JOHN: I can't leave my mother.

JULIE: You deserve your own life.

JOHN: That's not how it works for us.

JULIE: It's not how it works for *any* of us. But we have to make our own lives!

JOHN: Where would we go?

JULIE: Who cares, John? Let's just go.

JOHN: We both belong to Veenen Plaas. We'll drown out there.

JULIE: You said you had a plan.

JOHN: I do. But I can't leave my mum here.

JULIE: OK. So we take Christine with us. To the city. We – I don't know – start a hotel. Buy an old house and fix it up. I've always wanted to do that. Make something old and ugly – new. I'll deal with the guests. You can fix things. Christine runs the kitchen and makes the beds. We could

be a place with a story: The couple that ran away from
Veenen Plaas.

JOHN: It's a beautiful story. *(Indicating the sign over the door.)*
'The Weeping Farm.'

They laugh.

JULIE: What are we staying for? A pair of boots to polish and
an ancestor beneath the floor? My father's already got his
grave marked out next to my ma. And his parents. And
theirs. All the way back to the Voortrekkers[33]. There's a
spot reserved for me too – but they can give that red dust
to someone else. What are we staying for? Graves and soil?

JOHN: My mother wants to be buried here. She will never go.

JULIE: Then you must go without her. You're a man now,
John. Not a boy.

JOHN: *(Possibility is growing for him.)* How much for an old
house?

JULIE: How much do *you* have?

JOHN: Me? *(Laughs, stunned that she can even ask.)* I still owe
your father my next three wages. From when mum broke
the kitchen floor.

JULIE: John, *I* don't have anything. Until my father dies – I
don't even own this land.

*CHRISTINE enters the kitchen. JOHN and JULIE scatter – scrambling
for clothes.*

---

33 **pioneers** *(Afrikaans for 'those who go ahead'). Emigrants during the 1830s
and 1840s who left the British Cape Colony, migrating into the interior
Highveld, north of the Orange River in South Africa.*

CHRISTINE has a spade over her shoulder and a bucket in hand, filled with blood. She wears a torch tucked into her plastic apron and a shawl about her shoulders, against the dark morning cold. She watches them silently as they fumble with buttons and zips.

CHRISTINE: *(When they are still, she pours the blood into a nearby bucket.)* Diana is finished now miesie. I buried the puppies out beyond the field. By the windmill. I got up to do it before sunrise. With this heat…they would rot fast out there. Still no rain. Just light drops that mark the dust and make this old roof leak.

Looking out across the skies.

(Inscrutably.) Some children living in the karoo have never seen rain. They've seen the clouds roll in from the Kalahari, and they've heard the gysie[34] sing for three days. But nothing. Never seen a storm. It can bewitch you – the endless promise of rain.

Try to get some sleep, mies. I'll wake you when your father gets here.

Addressing her son.

Wena![35] I'll press your suit for church.

They are alone again. JULIE watches JOHN, who is pacing, mortified.

JULIE: John, what are you thinking?

JOHN: I'm thinking –
I have boots to clean.

JOHN picks up the boots and begins to polish.

---

34 *A small field cricket, common in the karoo, that is known to sing for up to three days prior to rainfall.*
35 **You!** *(isiXhosa)*

JULIE: We have to go. My father will be home soon.

JOHN: We're staying.

JULIE: We can't stay. Everything has changed.

JOHN: Nothing has changed. *(Bitter.)* Welcome to Mzantsi[36], Mies Julie. Where miracles leave us exactly where we began.

JULIE: But…you love me.

JOHN: *(Cold.)* So what?

JULIE: Since I was a girl. My dress in the tree. Me in a blanket. You drowning in the grain.

JOHN: You liked that. That I wanted to die for you?

JULIE: Yes.

JOHN: Why?

JULIE: Because I'm a woman.

JOHN: A boer – who wants my black skin on a wall.

JULIE: Don't do this.

JOHN: I can't help myself.

JULIE: Don't be cruel.

JOHN: You like it.

JULIE: You hate me.

---

36 **South Africa** *(from the isiXhosa word 'uMzantsi' meaning 'south'.)*

JOHN: No, Mies Julie. I don't hate you. You're a detail.

JULIE: You love me.

JOHN: I lied.

JULIE: The grain silo?

JOHN: Read it in a book by an Afrikaans poet. You people like sacrifice. As long as it's someone else's blood.

JULIE: You have no idea what love is.

JOHN: And you do? Your mother couldn't stand looking at you. Your father knows only the fist and the boot. The only love you've ever known is from the tired black hands of my mother.

JULIE: Jealous?

JOHN: No. I'm angry. There's a difference.

JULIE: Well grow the fuck up, John.

JOHN: *You* – can't even cook yourself a meal.
You depend on us for everything. We clean up your shit. Run your kitchens. Raise your children. Plough your fields. But still – like a child – you want.

JULIE: What? What do I want? Your stinking poverty? Your desperation?
Your rags?

He turns to leave. She runs after him.

JULIE: *(On her knees, her arms around him.)*
Please.

Please.

He shakes her off. She grabs him.

JOHN: What do you want from me?

He kisses her violently. She responds. He throws her to the floor, and sits.

Say it! What do you want?

She crawls to him, weeping, grasping at him. He lifts her to him and kisses her again. He throws her to the ground and stands. He kicks open her legs.

You want this?

He pulls her to her feet and shoves her – face first – over the table. He pulls her dress up, pushing himself into her brutally from behind.

This? You want this?

JULIE: *(Weeping.)* Yes! I want it.

He zips up and walks away. She is weeping.

Jou vokken vark![37]

JOHN: You don't get what you want anymore.
That's what has changed. There's freedom in that for both of us.

JULIE: Ek verstaan nie.[38]

---

37 **You fucking pig!** *(Afrikaans)*
38 **I don't understand.** *(Afrikaans)*

JOHN: Since I was a boy – going hunting with your father at dawn, carrying his gun, being his 'best boy' – I've watched him take what he wants and still behave like he's owed.

JULIE: John, I'm just a boer –

JOHN: …With nothing on the table, who now wants to cut a deal.

(She spits in his face.)

JULIE: A kaffir! Who will do anything to get his hand in the jar.

JOHN: And I liked getting my hand in the jar. Making you bleed. *(Shoving his hand between her legs.)*

This is my blood covenant, Voortrekker Girl. Running down your thigh.

He grabs the wine and drinks straight from the bottle.

JULIE: That is my father's best wine. When he finds out…

JOHN: What? That I fucked his daughter? Or drank his wine?

JULIE: A kaffir will always be a kaffir.

JOHN: And a bitch will always be a bitch.

JULIE: I can't believe I let you touch me.

JOHN: I didn't touch you. I fucked you! You're full of my seed. A harvest I planted for the future last night.

He sits at the table with his feet up.

Tell me, Mies Julie. What if you're carrying my child?

227

She drops to her knees in horror.

Then this land will return to the rightful owners.

JULIE: So this… This is your revenge?

JOHN: No!
This is restitution.
Of body and soil.

JULIE: My God. Wat is jy?[39]

JOHN: A man. With a plan.

JULIE: Be careful. The nest you have your hand in, is a black mamba's.

JOHN: You're not a snake. You're the past. A sad, empty-handed boer still trying to be powerful.

JULIE: And you are just a KAFFIR! STAAN OP WANEER JY MET MY PRAAT – JOU FOKKEN PLAAS KAFFIR![40]
You'll never be anything but a kaffir. Good for cleaning boots.

(She weeps for sometime. He watches her.)

I could have loved you.

JOHN: You don't love me. You never will.

JULIE: Why not?

JOHN: Because love is not possible in this mess.

---

39 **What are you?** *(Afrikaans)*
40 **Stand up when you are talking to me, you fucking farm kaffir!**
(Afrikaans)

JULIE: What if I do? What if I have since I was a girl?

(She holds him. He yields. They hold one another. He pulls away.)

JOHN: Stop it!

JULIE: Why?

JOHN: You want me dead. I will not die for you.

JULIE: I love you. I believed you when you said you do.

JOHN: I did.

JULIE: When did you stop?

JOHN: When you gave yourself to me.
   This morning – when I saw my mother's trembling hands.

JULIE: Why? Why does it have to be like this?

JOHN: I don't know, Julie.

JULIE: We're all so scared.

JOHN: Yes.

JULIE: Hit me.

JOHN: What?

JULIE: Hurt me. Please.

JOHN: No.

JULIE: HIT ME.

She beats her arms, her face – savagely. He grabs her.

JOHN: Stop! Julie stop!

She weeps. He holds her. He whispers.

I'm sorry. I'm sorry.

JULIE: *(Pushing him away.)* Pour me a drink.

He does. She grabs the bottle from his hand and chugs.

My ma always tried to fit in here with the other boere[41]
tannies. But they were always harder, crueler. Having
their hair and nails done on Fridays like they were going
to battle. If you are sensitive out here in this arid land –
you don't make it. They often found her in her nightie
– standing by the power station – listening in the dark.
My father told me once that's what killed her. She
listened. To what's beneath. If you're tender out here –
you drown.

She gulps more wine from the bottle. JOHN pulls it away gently.

JOHN: Don't drink anymore, Julie.

JULIE: He lost patience. She would hit him. And sometimes he
would hit her back. Those were the mornings she would
come to breakfast looking calm. With bruises from his fists.
My ma was always elsewhere.

JOHN: My mother was always with you.

JULIE: I know.

I love this farm.
It's all I know.

---

41 **farmer's wives** *(Literally, Afrikaans for 'aunties' but connotes 'wives' here)*

JOHN: What do you love?

JULIE: Everything. The space. The silence. When I was sent to boarding school – I thought I would die.

JOHN: It's not yours to love.

JULIE: Says who? What makes it less mine than yours? Your black skin?

JOHN: My people are buried here. Beneath this floor.

JULIE: So are mine. Out there beneath the willow trees. Three generations back. Where the fuck do I go?

JOHN: That's not my problem.
They stole it.
Your people.

JULIE: Fok jou.[42] So did yours. From the First here. How far back do you want to go?

JOHN: Let's just say your people did things to keep it that can never be excused.

They are both silent.

Love me, Mies Julie. Love the land. Love that old windmill out there. But we will never be yours.

JULIE: A boere tannie once threw hot soup at her for saying we don't belong here. She just laughed. Said when people turn violent – you know you've told the truth. There's something to be said for violence. Lets you know where you stand.

---

42 **Fuck you.** *(Afrikaans)*

JOHN: That's why you hit Baas Jan with the sjambok[43]?

JULIE: What did you see that day?

JOHN: You on your knees. Him forcing himself like an animal into your mouth. Did that feel honest?

JULIE: It was his finest moment.

JOHN: Why?

JULIE: He was being true.

JOHN: You hate yourself, Julie.

JULIE: No, John. I hate you.

JOHN: Why? You have everything of mine.

JULIE: I have nothing. Don't you see?

JOHN: Mother.
    Body.
    Land.

JULIE: Die with me.

JOHN: Die?

JULIE: Let's start new.

JOHN: I'm going to bed. Turn the light off when you leave.

He turns to go.

JULIE: Not so fast, fucker! You owe me.

---

43 *A whip of cured leather, capable of inflicting great pain and damage to the skin.*

JOHN: Owe *you*?

JULIE: You don't use me and throw me away like that.

JOHN: You boere. You take and take. But when something is taken – you want to burn the house down. You complain what a mess everything is out there. Who made the fucking mess? The party is over. We'll clean up your shit as usual. Just go.

JULIE: Where? This is my home. My great grandfather built it with his bare hands.

JOHN: Your great grandfather was a squatter. Take this shack and build it somewhere else.

JULIE: A squatter? Is that what you just said?

JOHN: He who moves onto open land to gain title. I read. Remember?

JULIE: Tell that to my father.

JOHN: He cries war on those doing exactly what your ancestors did.

JULIE: We own the deeds to this land.

JOHN: From whom? The man who first took what never belonged to him?

He makes for the door.

JULIE: Walk away and I will scream rape.

JOHN stops dead in his tracks.

I am full of your seed. I have evidence. I bled.

JOHN: Of course – this is where desire ends. The white daughter crying rape on the black man. So that her father can accept her fucking him.

JULIE: You will be in jail by tonight if he does not put a bullet in your head first.

JOHN: Remember – your father promised you a bullet in the head too. So here we are: Two kaffirs. Doomed to die.

JULIE: I don't know how to be anymore.

JOHN: I know.

JULIE: I need you, John.

JOHN: I don't need you, Julie.

JULIE: Yes – you do.

I may be carrying your child. If I disappear – you are back to cleaning boots.

They are both silent.

My father has money in his safe.

JOHN: And a gun. I know.

JULIE: I know the code to the lock.

He looks at her.

(Her hand on her belly.) Let's go until the storm passes. Maybe we can return someday with a child who walks with all our ancestors in the shadows – who lay claim to Veenen Plaas.

JOHN: Go. Get what we need.

JULIE: You'll come with me?

JOHN: Get what we need and come back here.

JULIE: Speak kindly to me.

JOHN: This is what orders tastes like. What we swallow everyday. Go.

JULIE exits. JOHN sits with his head in his hands. CHRISTINE enters. She is immaculately dressed in her Church uniform. She holds a Bible in her left hand, and JOHN's suit on a hanger in her right. She lays the suit flat on the table.)

CHRISTINE: Get ready for Church.

JOHN: I'm tired.

CHRISTINE: Too tired for God?
Look at me.
LOOK AT ME!

She suddenly slaps him brutally in the face.

What have you done? We have nothing. Nowhere else to go!

JOHN: Mama, there is more! More to life than slave wages and scrubbing a floor!

CHRISTINE: Is that so?

JOHN: Why just accept?

Why accept scrubbing that floor for the rest of your life?

Freedom is not worth shit! As long as we must pay honour to ancestors that bind us to this dead land where nothing grows!

She holds up her hand in front of him – palm and fingertips facing toward him. She is silent.

What is it, ma?

CHRISTINE: No fingerprints.

JOHN: What?

CHRISTINE: When I went to vote for the first time – 18 years ago – they needed fingerprints for identification. But they're gone. I lost them. Rubbed them smooth, cleaning this floor! These walls! That child!

JOHN: Ma –

CHRISTINE: They told me they would make a plan for me. Said there were other maids with the same problem. No identity. But I never went back. What's gone is gone, and can never be reclaimed.

JOHN is silent. He covers his face with his hands. He feels like he may weep and it will never end.

Now get dressed for church. And when we come back – there is work to be done.

JOHN: I want more, ma. I want what belongs to us.

CHRISTINE: Our jobs belong to us. It's more than most people have. Do the boots. Be grateful. Get dressed. Go to church on Sundays.

As long as those bones lie beneath this floor – that's how we get to stay near our ancestors on this land.

I'm waiting outside.

CHRISTINE exits. UKHOKO is slowly circling the periphery, watching JOHN – who agonizes over this decision. He removes his gumboots and puts the jacket from the suit on. Upstage, as though outside the kitchen, JULIE takes down the birdcage and tenderly covers it with fabric.

JULIE: Ek's reg.[44]

(She has entered holding a small bag, the shotgun strapped to her back and the birdcage.)

JOHN: You're a mess.

JULIE: How?

JOHN: Your face is dirty.

JULIE: *(Rubbing her face.)* Die son is op.[45]

JOHN: How much do you have?

JULIE: Enough.

JULIE puts the rifle and the birdcage on the table.

JOHN: What is that?

JULIE: My bird. I can't leave her behind.

JOHN: We can't take it. Are you mad?

---

44 **I'm ready.** *(Afrikaans)*
45 **The sun is up.** *(Afrikaans)*

JULIE: I'd rather she were dead than alone.

JOHN: Give it to me. I'll do it.

JULIE takes the bird out of the cage and kisses it tenderly.

JOHN grabs it and crushes it in his hands. JULIE screams. He throws it in the nearby bucket.

JULIE: *(Devastated.)* I'd like to see your blood and brains on a wall.

CHRISTINE enters – Bible in hand.

JULIE: Hold me, Christine. Like when I was small.

CHRISTINE: *(Cradling her.)* Sssh. The storm is breaking. There will be rain coming soon.

JULIE: We must run away before my father gets home.

CHRISTINE: I cleaned the blood off these walls myself. The madam sat in this chair. Sunday morning. Put the master's rifle under her chin. You found her here in this kitchen.

Came running to get me from the veldt. You kept asking me what you had done wrong. I said: 'Nothing, little one. It's not your fault. It's not your fault'.

JULIE: Christine. Me and John are going away to open a hotel. Will you come with us, ma?

CHRISTINE looks at JOHN stunned.

CHRISTINE: I'm going nowhere. Except to church. And then home to clean this house.

JULIE: Christine – we could be a family.

CHRISTINE: *A family?* You *believe* that, mies?

JULIE: I don't know, Christine. I don't know what I believe anymore.

JOHN: Ma – I was never going to leave you.

CHRISTINE: You were going to do what?

JOHN: Take back what belongs to us.

CHRISTINE: You disgrace your ancestors.

JOHN: *(A cry from his soul.)* Mama, I'm tired of waiting!

CHRISTINE: What do you know about waiting? You were born ten minutes ago.

JOHN: *(Brutally.)* You are going to keep scrubbing that floor until you die.

CHRISTINE: I will wait. Until this house turns to dust. Until this floor turns to sand. Until the waters rise and it all floats away. I can't break it open and set them free. I have tried. So I wait. These roots are my hands. And beneath these stones – my blood is warm.

JOHN: We take it back ourselves. Or we leave.

CHRISTINE: Get ready for church.

JOHN: They took our land and handed us the Bible.

I'm not going to Church. Ever again.

He grabs her Bible and throws it brutally. CHRISTINE drops to her knees, broken. She holds the Bible. She rises and tries to compose herself.

CHRISTINE: I will meet you there when you are finished with this mess.

I trust you, my boy.

CHRISTINE leaves. JOHN is sitting on the floor, devastated.

JULIE: Can you see a way out of all this? An end for the whole thing?

JOHN: *(He can barely speak.)* Go. There's no other way.

JULIE: I've nowhere to go.

JOHN: Then stay and fight. You will lose.

If you are lucky – my child is in your womb and your children will have a place on Veenen Plaas.

In one move – she grabs the rifle and has it pointed at JOHN's head.

JULIE: You think I love you, Kaffir boy? That I'm going to carry your black child under my heart. Feed it with my blood? Give it your name? Wash your socks and underpants; cook your food; raise your children? Be your kaffir! And when my father dies, your black child inherits this land? Is that what you had in mind?

JOHN: It's a good deal. More than your children deserve.

JULIE: You have no capital. No skills. You're a slave.

JOHN: Yes. I have nothing. That's the legacy your people leave.

A nation of grown men and women – good for nothing but cleaning boots.

JOHN seizes the gun.

But it will be our boots we clean. On our own land.

JULIE scrambles for the sickle JOHN was sharpening the night before.

JULIE: I will die before I let you take this Farm.

They square up. Gun and sickle.

JOHN: So here we are.
    Free at last.
    No longer master and slave.
    Just two people in a kitchen.
    Fighting for our lives.

She drops to her knees. He has the gun aimed at her head.

JULIE: The Valley of Desolation. That's where I would run to in the mornings. After she died. Standing at the foot of all that rock. Volcanoes and erosions made it over millions of years. Before any of us were here.

Raising the sickle.

I'm a Boer, John. We don't go down without a fight.

JOHN: I can't save you from yourself, Julie.

JULIE: I haven't got a self. I haven't got a thought I don't get from my father. I haven't a passion I didn't get from my

241

mother. So how can it be my fault? Who is responsible for the wrong? What does it matter to us who is?

JOHN: Julie…

JULIE: You think my body your restitution? My womb your land grab?

JOHN: You don't even know if that child exists.

JULIE: But if I love you again, John – it will. And I'm not taking any chances. Here is *my* blood vow.

She pushes the sickle between her legs, and thrusts the blade upwards into her womb.

A gush of blood. He grabs her.

JOHN: Julie!

He cradles her and carries her to the table. He continues to hold her. She is bleeding profusely.

JULIE: There is mist over the valley in the morning when I wake. It smells like fire. And I realize it's smoke.

JOHN: Julie…

JULIE: Everyone is crying. They are going farm to farm. Burning our fields. Our homes. Scorching the earth. We stand. In silence. Ash in our hair as our farms burn.

JOHN: These memories are not yours, Julie.

JULIE: In the Camps, I watch my children fade and fly away. I bury them at night when no one can see me cry. They sing. The dead children. Welcoming each other through the night.

JOHN: These memories…

JULIE: Are buried out there beneath the willows.

Bury me with them. In the red earth.

Ssh! He's here. Outside.

She is dead. The fan stops turning. He holds her. He tears open her dress and weeps into her breasts. He falls to his knees.

He sits at the table, head in hands. He stands suddenly, panicked. He covers JULIE with his scarf.

He moves to the boots he has been polishing all his life. He puts them on.

He picks up the gun in his right hand and the sickle in his left.

He lowers his head for a moment – overcome.

JOHN: It's easy.

He steels himself.

Just pretend you're him.

Lights shift.

CHRISTINE is alone, on her knees, cleaning the blood off the floor.

UKHOKHO sings and plays her traditional Xhosa bow.

Lights fade – until nothing but the tree stump and roots remain.

Ends.

WWW.OBERONBOOKS.COM